Berlin Apartments

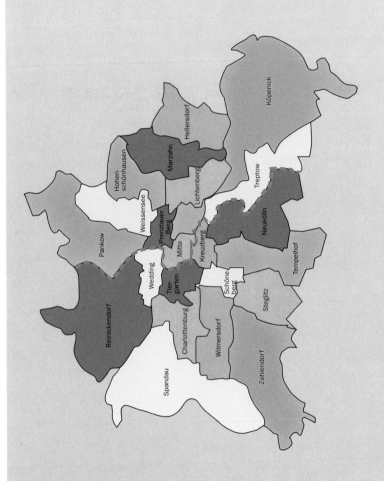

The districts of Berlin

▬ ▬ ▬ ▬ Previous route of the Berlin Wall

Köpenick

Hellersdorf

Marzahn

Hohen-
schönhausen

Lichtenberg

Treptow

Weissensee

Prenzlauer
Berg

Neukölln

Pankow

Mitte

Kreuzberg

Tempelhof

Wedding

Tier-
garten

Schöne-
berg

Reinickendorf

Steglitz

Charlottenburg

Wilmersdorf

Zehlendorf

Spandau

Berlin Apartments

teNeues

Editor in chief: Paco Asensio
Editores: Haike Falkenberg, Cynthia Reschke
Editorial coordination and texts: Anja Jaworsky
Art director: Mireia Casanovas Soley
Layout: Gisela Legares Gili
Copyediting: Francesc Bombí-Vilaseca, Sabine Würfel
French translation: Leïla Marçot
English translation: Matthew Clarke
Spanish translation: Almudena Sasiain

Published by teNeues Publishing Group

teNeues Publishing Company
16 West 22nd Street, New York, NY 10010, US
Tel.: 001-212-627-9090, fax: 001-212-627-9511

teNeues Book Division
Neuer Zollhof 1
40221 Düsseldorf, Germany
Tel.: 0049-(0)211-994597-0, fax: 0049-(0)211-994597-40

teNeues Publishing UK Ltd.
Aldwych House, 71/91 Aldwych
London WC2B 4HN, UK

www.teneues.com

ISBN: 3-8238-5596-4

Editorial project:

© 2002 LOFT Publications
Domènech 9, 2-2
08012 Barcelona, Spain
Tel.: 0034 932 183 099
Fax: 0034 932 370 060
e-mail: loft@loftpublications.com
www.loftpublications.com

If you would like to suggest projects for inclusion in our next
volumes, please e-mail details to us at: loft@loftpublications.com

Die Deutsche Bibliothek – CIP-Einheitsaufnahme
Ein Titeldatensatz für diese Publikation ist bei der Deutschen
Bibliothek erhältlich.

Printed by: Gràfiques Anman, Sabadell, Spain

September 2002

Berlin

Berlin

Einleitung

Wohl in keiner anderen Stadt Europas hat sich in den letzten Jahrzehnten ein so großer Wandel vollzogen wie in Berlin. Fast kann man behaupten, dass diese Stadt unter all den europäischen Groß- und Hauptstädten ein Sonderdasein genießt und ihr Charme und Reiz sowohl in ihrer Lebendigkeit als auch in dem sich ständig wandelnden Gesicht und Ambiente besteht, die Anziehungskraft anderer europäischer Großstädte hingegen eher darauf beruht, dass Bewohner und Besucher ein spezifisches Bild dieser Städte in sich tragen.

Das Berliner „Viertelleben"

Berlin ist groß und dies vor allem in seiner flächenmäßigen Ausdehnung. Die 3,5 Millionen Einwohner leben auf 900 km^2 verteilt (statistisch gesehen verfügt jeder Einwohner über einen Lebensraum von 32,9 m^2) und dies ist wohl auch der ausschlaggebende Grund dafür, dass sich traditionell ein starkes „Viertelleben" entwickelt hat. Viele Berliner beschränken ihr gesellschaftliches und berufliches Leben auf einen bestimmten Radius um ihren Wohnort herum, denn das Lieblingscafé ist gleich nebenan, die Stammkneipe um die Ecke, und eine gute Infrastruktur mit Einkaufszentren und kleinen Läden ist in allen Vierteln vorhanden.

Die Viertel

Insgesamt gibt es 23 Viertel, in diesem Buch werden jedoch vor allem Wohnungen vorgestellt, die im unmittelbaren Stadtzentrum liegen. Dies sind:

Charlottenburg

Der heute eher gutbürgerliche Bezirk Charlottenburg wurde in den 80er Jahren beliebt, als durch die ersten Hausbesetzer die Aufmerksamkeit auf ihn gelenkt wurde. Ganz plötzlich begann man rege in die baufälligen und heruntergekommenen Altbauten zu investieren und schon nach kurzer Zeit stiegen die Mietpreise an. Zu Zeiten der Mauer bildete der Bezirk zudem die Stadtmitte Westberlins und der berühmte Kurfürstendamm und die dortige Kneipen- und Barszene florierten. Heute erinnert man sich hier ein wenig wehmütig an diese Zeiten zurück, als man nicht mit einer Vielzahl neuer Attraktionen konkurrieren musste. Das Theater des Westens und das Schloss Charlottenburg sind zwar weiterhin beliebte Touristenziele, die Partymeile hat sich jedoch in die Bezirke Mitte und Prenzlauer Berg verlagert.

Mitte

In den 20er Jahren war der Bezirk Mitte der kulturelle Dreh- und Angelpunkt der Stadt. Durch den Mauerbau und die Teilung Deutschlands bildete er über Jahrzehnte ein unzugängliches Grenzgebiet zwischen Ost- und Westberlin. Nach dem Mauerfall bot das ungenutzte Brachland ein riesiges Flächenpotential und zog Großinvestoren, renommierte Architekten und Designer zur Verwirklichung interessanter Bauprojekte an. In den letzten Jahren hat sich dieser Bezirk nun erneut zum pulsierenden Zentrum der Stadt entwickelt und über Jahre konnte man hier die größte Baustelle Europas bewundern. Hunderte von Baukränen und unfertige Neubauten prägten das Straßenbild. Der Bau des Sony Centers von Stararchitekt Helmut Jahn und des Debishauses von Daimler Chrysler durch Renzo Piano sind einige der herausragenden neuen „Wahrzeichen" der Stadt. Rund um die Auguststraße, Sophien- und Heckmannhöfe ist eine Kunstmeile mit Galerien und Szenetreffs entstanden und durch die Bebauung des Pariser Platzes wurde auch das jahrzehntelang nicht zur Durchfahrt freigegebene Brandenburger Tor aus seiner Isolation im ehemaligen Grenzstreifen befreit.

Prenzlauer Berg

Im ehemaligen Ostberliner Bezirk Prenzlauer Berg hatten sich schon zu DDR-Zeiten viele Intellektuelle und Künstler gesammelt und nach dem Mauerfall zog es dann auch vor allem die experimentelle Szene dort hin. Die vielen leerstehenden Wohnungen, Keller und Gewerbebauten wurden einfach besetzt und zu Wohnzwecken, Bars oder auch anderweitig umfunktioniert. Sie boten eine hervorragende Möglichkeit, unkonventionelle Ideen zu verwirklichen. Heute ist aus dem traditionellen Arbeiterviertel mit seinen florierenden Cafes, Bars und Galerien ein angesagtes Viertel zum Wohnen und Ausgehen geworden.

Schöneberg

Der Bezirk Schöneberg ist mit seinen kleinen Läden, Kiezflair und dem Charme großer Altbauwohnungen ein traditionell beliebter Wohnort.

Kreuzberg

Im Bezirk Kreuzberg, wo jahrzehntelang die Hausbesetzer- und alternative Szene auf sich aufmerksam machte, ist es ruhiger geworden. Früher gab es hier den sogenannten Bezirk SO 36 (Viertelbezeichnung, die sich aus der Lage Südost und den Endzahlen der Postleitzahl zusammensetzt), wo die U-Bahn nicht mehr weiterfuhr, weil die Endstation auch gleichzeitig die Mauergrenze darstellte. Heute wird das Straßenbild wieder mehr vom bunten Treiben der großen und seit vielen Generationen hier ansässigen Türkengemeinde geprägt. Die zentrale Lage, die vielen schönen Altbauwohnungen und die immer noch rege Kneipenkultur machen jedoch auch diesen Bezirk interessant für viele Neuinvestitionen.

Friedrichshain

Der ehemalige Arbeiterbezirk Friedrichshain ist 13 Jahre nach dem

Mauerfall vor allem zum Zufluchtsort all derer geworden, die durch die Milliarden-baustellen und Reformen aus den Bezirken Mitte und Prenzlauer Berg vertrieben wurden, u.a. weil ihnen diese Bezirke ganz einfach zu teuer geworden sind. Durch die Spree vom Stadtteil Kreuzberg getrennt und nur über eine einzige Verkehrsverbin-dung, die Oberbaumbrücke, zu erreichen, sind hier die Mietpreise noch immer er-schwinglich und bieten einen idealen Nährboden und Lebensraum für eine neue Sub-kultur.

Zehlendorf

Zehlendorf liegt im Südwesten der Stadt, ein wenig außerhalb des unmittelbaren Stadtzentrums. Inmitten von viel Grün und am Rande der Stadterholungsgebiete Wannsee und Grunewald mit Wäldern, Parkanlagen und zahlreichen Seen hat sich in dieser bevorzugten Lage vor allem ein betuchteres Publikum und die Elite der Archi-tekten und Designerszene niedergelassen, die sich in schmucken Einfamilienhäu-sern oder edlen Villen von der Hektik der Stadt erholten.

Der treibende Impuls der Stadt

Mit dem Mauerfall und der Wiederbelebung der alten Ostbezirke ist viel Bewegung in die Stadt gekommen. Vor allem Neuhinzugezogene und junge Leute zieht es dorthin, wo sich etwas „bewegt". Schon immer jedoch gingen wichtige Impulse von der florie-renden Berliner Subkultur aus. Wie bei einem Katz-Maus-Spiel verlagerten sich belieb-te und angesagte Wohnorte dorthin, wo sich gerade die experimentelle und alternative Kunst- und Musikszene installiert hatte. Investoren spürten die neuen In-Bezirke auf und sobald dann die Renovierungs- und Verschönerungsarbeiten im Viertel begannen, flüchtete die Szene auf der Suche nach neuen Nischen in andere Bezirke.

Was macht Berlin so attraktiv?

Berlin ist nicht wirklich kosmopolit, sondern hat sich trotz Metropolenfieber nach dem Mauerfall seinen Eigencharakter bewahrt. In vieler Hinsicht wirkt es fast provinziell, doch schon immer war es ein Ort von großer politischer und kultureller Aktivität. Die legendären 20er Jahre und das zu jener Zeit florierende Kabarett und Varieté sind für immer in die Kulturgeschichte eingegangen, und viele berühmte Architekten, Künst-ler und Wissenschaftler wie Walter Gropius, Hans Scharoun, Bruno Taut, Emil Fah-renkamp, Hans Pelzig, Martin Wagner, Max Liebermann, Max Beckmann, Bertolt Brecht, Arnold Zweig, Kurt Tucholsky etc. wirkten in der Stadt. Die besondere „In-sellage" während der Teilung Deutschlands haben den Eigencharakter der Berliner noch verstärkt. Viel Lebensqualität bieten außer dem schier grenzenlosen kulturellen Angebot die vielen Grünanlagen sowohl im Stadtzentrum als auch in der unmittelba-ren Umgebung der Stadt. Fast ein Viertel der Stadtfläche sind Wälder, Seen und Flüs-se, die für Erholung und viele Freizeitmöglichkeiten sorgen. Im Zentrum ist vor allem der Tiergartenpark ein beliebter Freizeitort, der sich im Sommer des öfteren in einen riesigen sonntäglichen Grillplatz verwandelt.

Die jüngste Stadtgeschichte

Historisch betrachtet sind mit dem Namen Berlin glorreiche Zeiten, aber auch viele Niedergänge verbunden. Die jüngere Stadtgeschichte wurde vor allem durch die Folgen des 2. Weltkrieges bestimmt, nach dem Berlin zunächst einem riesigen Trümmerhaufen glich. Über 600.000 Wohnungen (jedes 3. Wohnhaus) waren zerstört und nur durch die mühsame Arbeit der sogenannten „Trümmerfrauen" sind der Stadt eine große Anzahl von Gründerzeitbauten (1870-1900) erhalten geblieben.

Der Mauerbau 1961 zwang der Stadt eine jahrzehntelange schmerzliche Teilung auf und als am 09.11.1989 die Grenzen wieder geöffnet wurden, stand man vor einer Stadt mit zwei Gesichtern. Sowohl in Ost- als auch in Westberlin hatte die stark zerstörte Infrastruktur nach dem 2. Weltkrieg einen Wiederaufbau gefordert, doch während man im sozialistisch regierten Ostteil der Stadt z. B. beim Wohnungsbau vor allem nach Quantität strebte und die sogenannten „Plattenbausiedlungen" im Fertigbaustil das architektonische Bild beherrschten, wurden in West-Berlin Modelle zur Innenstadtsanierung erarbeitet und anspruchsvolle Neubauten errichtet.

Mit dem Mauerfall begann eine Zeit schier grenzenloser und kontinuierlicher Veränderung, die Menschen aus allen Teilen der Welt anzog, um an der Euphorie- und Aufbruchstimmung teilzuhaben. Der Beschluss, Berlin erneut zur Hauptstadt und Metropole zu machen, ließ die Stadt über Jahre im Bau- und Planungsfieber pulsieren. 13 Jahre nach dem Mauerfall ist es nun wieder ruhiger geworden und man beginnt Bilanz zu ziehen. Doch die Wiedervereinigung ist auf vielen Gebieten noch nicht vollzogen und längst nicht alle Möglichkeiten und Ideen sind verwirklicht, so dass man der Stadt auch weiterhin eine spannende Zukunft in Aussicht stellen kann.

Dieses Buch soll einen Einblick in die vielseitige Berliner Wohnkultur schaffen und zeigt sowohl private Domizile, die von renommierten Architekten und Designern wie Stefan Sterf, Heinz Hellermann, Barkow-Leibinger, die Grollwitz Zappe Architekten, die Peanutz Architekten, die Architekten Hoyer & Schindele, etc. gestaltet wurden als auch Wohnungen, die mit viel Eigeninitiative und begrenzten finanziellen Mitteln entstanden sind, aber den so typischen Eigencharakter der Berliner widerspiegeln. Die Lebendigkeit und Vielfältigkeit der Stadt manifestiert sich im privaten Wohnbereich mit modernsten High Tech, Loft- und Minimalismuswohnungen bis hin zu individuellen Künstlerwohnungen und herrschaftlichen Gründerzeitwohnungen oder der Flucht ins Eigenheim in Form eines Einfamilienhauses im Grünen.

Introduction

There is probably no city in Europe that has undergone such a spectacular transformation as Berlin in the last few decades. It could be said that Berlin stands out from other European cities and capitals because its special charm is derived from its striking energy and its constant changes in appearance and atmosphere; in contrast, the attraction of other great European cities tends to reside in a specific, immutable image treasured by its inhabitants and visitors.

The neighbourhood life of Berlin

Berlin is a big city, particularly in terms of its geographical extension. Its 3.5 million inhabitants are spread out over 28 square miles (statistically speaking, each inhabitant has 340 square feet). This probably explains why individual neighbourhoods have always developed such an intense life of their own. Many Berliners confine their social and professional life to a specific radius around their home, as their favorite café is next door, their regular bar is on the corner and every neighbourhood has a good network of shopping centers and small stores.

The neighbourhoods

There are 23 neighbourhoods in all. Most of the homes shown in this book are situated in the city center. The most central neighbourhoods are described below.

Charlottenburg

This neighbourhood, now somewhat middle-class and well-to-do, began to experience a boom in the 1980s, when the first squatters brought it to the attention of the public. Money suddenly began to be invested in its dilapidated old buildings, and the rents soon started to go up. During the time of the Wall this neighbourhood was also the hub of West Berlin and the bars and nightspots on the famous Kurfürstendamm became fashionable. These days locals recall with a certain nostalgia those times as there was not so much competition from other new attractions. Although the Western Theatre and the Charlottenburg Palace are still major tourist sights, the city's night life has moved to the neighbourhoods of Mitte and Prenzlauer Berg.

Mitte

In the 1920s Mitte was the city's cultural center. The construction of the Wall and the division of Germany reduced it to an inaccessible frontier zone between the East and West for decades. After the opening up of the Wall, this neglected strip of no-man's-land was ripe for exploitation and it attracted major developers, as well as famous architects and designers interested in bringing exciting building projects to life. Recently Mitte has once again become the city's nerve center, and for many years it boasted the most extensive building works in the whole of Europe, with cranes and construction sites forming an integral part of the landscape. The city's most outstanding new "symbols" include the Sony Center complex designed by the famous architect Helmut Jahn and the Debishaus building, the Daimler Chrysler headquarters built by Renzo Piano. Auguststrasse and the Sofia and Heckmann courtyards have evolved into an area devoted to art, with galleries and cultural meeting points. The redevelopment of the Paris Platz has delivered the Brandenburg Gate – now open to traffic once again – from the isolation that its status as a frontier zone had previously bestowed upon it.

Prenzlauer Berg

The East Berlin neighbourhood of Prenzlauer Berg was already a haven for intellectuals and artists in the days of the German Democratic Republic. So, after the demolition of the Wall, devotees of the experimental scene moved here. Countless apartments, basements and commercial premises were squatted without any further ado and done up as homes, bars and other types of venues. These buildings offered extraordinary possibilities for bringing unconventional ideas to fruition. Today this traditionally working-class neighbourhood, with its thriving cafés, bars and galleries, has become highly appreciated as both a place to live and a good source of night-time entertainment.

Schöneberg

The Schöneberg neighbourhood, with its small stores, its distinctive, slightly decadent atmosphere and its charming old buildings, has also grown to be prized as a good place to live. Moreover, its array of cafés, bars and restaurants create a very lively atmosphere, both by day and by night.

Kreuzberg

For decades the squatters and other members of the underground focussed attention onto the neighbourhood of Kreuzberg but these days it is somewhat quieter. The eastern part of Kreuzberg used to be known as "neighbourhood SO 36" (SO for its southeasterly position and 36 for the final digits of its postcode); the subway came to a halt here, as the last stop coincided with the Wall. Nowadays Kreuzberg is mainly characterised by the colour and energy of the large Turkish community, which has been settled here for generations. Its central position, large number of old buildings and the continuing liveliness of its nightlife all mean that this neighbourhood still retains its appeal for new development projects.

Friedrichshain

Thirteen years after the demolition of the Wall, the old working-class neighbourhood of Friedrichshain has become the main refuge for people fleeing from Mitte and Prenzlauer Berg after they grew too expensive on account of the lavish conversions and building works. The river Spree separates it from the neighbourhood of Kreuzberg, and the only means of intercommunication is the Oberbaum bridge. The rents are still affordable, offering the ideal context for the emergence of a new subculture.

Zehlendorf

Amid woods, parks and a number of lakes, Zehlendorf lies to the south-west of Berlin, some way from the center, in open countryside next to the green belts of Wannsee and Grunewald. The inhabitants of this smart neighbourhood are mainly wealthy and include the cream of the world of architecture and design, who escape the hubbub of the city in elegant family houses and imposing mansions.

The dynamics of the city

The demolition of the Wall and the reactivation of the economies of the old neighbourhoods in the East have led to many changes. The neighbourhoods with the most life and activity are particularly attractive to young people and new arrivals. However, Berlin's fertile subculture has always played a large part in establishing which neighbourhoods are in fashion: one area drops off as the alternative cultural scene takes root in another district. Developers closely follow the trail of these newly fashionable neighbourhoods, and as soon as the conversions and smartening-up begins then the cultural focus turns to new spots in other neighbourhoods.

What makes Berlin such an attractive city?

Berlin is not really a cosmopolitan city. Despite the metropolitan fever that has taken over the city after the demolition of the Wall, the city has kept its own highly distinctive character. In many respects it is almost provincial but yet it has always been distinguished by its great political and cultural activity. The legendary 1920s and the night-time cabarets and revues that were all the rage at the time have now gone down in history. Many famous architects, artists and scientists – such as Walter Gropius, Hans Scharoun, Bruno Taut, Emil Fahrenkamp, Hans Pelzig, Martin Wagner, Max Liebermann, Max Beckmann, Bertolt Brecht, Arnold Zweig and Kurt Tucholsky – have left their mark on the city. When Germany was divided, its special geographical position as an "island" further strengthened the character of Berlin and its inhabitants. Apart from its almost unlimited cultural attractions, the numerous parks, both in the center and on the outskirts, greatly enhance the quality of living. Almost a quarter of Berlin's total surface area is covered by woods, lakes and rivers, offering a chance to relax, as well as plenty of opportunities to practice outdoor leisure activities. In the city center, the most popular retreat is the Tiergarten, a park studded with trees which is the perfect place for a summertime barbecue.

Berlin's recent history

Historically speaking, the city of Berlin has lived through golden ages but it has also known periods of sharp decline. The consequences of the Second World War have had a direct effect on its most recent history. Firstly, the city was reduced to a heap of rubble. More than 600,000 homes (or one building in every three) were destroyed. Thanks to the huge effort of the so-called "women of the the ruins", it proved possible to preserve a large number of buildings built in the Gründerzeit or years of speculation (1870-1900). Then the construction of the Wall led to decades of painful division. On November 9 1989, when the frontier was reopened once again, Berlin presented two very different faces. After the Second World War, the devastation suffered by both East and West was on such a huge scale that reconstruction became an urgent priority. However, while in the eastern part of the city, under Communist rule, the approach to rebuilding was based on quantity and the so-called Plattenbausiedlungen (enormous, uniform prefabricated blocks that dominated the architectural landscape), West Berlin benefited from urban replanning projects in the center and the guiding principle for new buildings was quality.

The demolition of the Wall gave rise to a period of continuous and unlimited change. The city attracted people from all over the world, eager to participate in those moments of euphoria and transformation. The decision to make Berlin the German capital once again plunged the city into a frenzy of planning and reconstruction that lasted years. Thirteen years after the disappearance of the Wall, the rhythm of Berlin has become somewhat more subdued and a period of reflection is now underway. However, German reunification has not been totally completed in many fields and many schemes are still waiting to be implemented. So, there is no doubt that Berlin still has an exciting future ahead of it.

This book seeks to give an impression of Berlin's rich urban culture. It presents private homes converted and decorated by renowned individual architects and designers – Stefan Sterf, Heinz Hellermann, Barkow-Leibinger – or by prestigious firms like Grollwitz Zappe, Peanutz, Hoyer & Schindele, but it also includes homes refurbished through the efforts and initiative of their residents on limited budgets – a perfect reflection of the spirit of Berlin. This city's dynamism and variety in terms of lifestyles and private spaces is apparent in the wide range of alternatives, from minimalist lofts and apartments equipped with the latest technological advances to artists' homes with their special atmosphere; from old late-nineteenth century mansion apartments to family houses in leafy areas on the outskirts, refuges from the bustle of the center.

Introduction

Il n'y a sans doute aucune autre ville d'Europe qui ait connu une métamorphose aussi spectaculaire que celle de Berlin au cours de ces dix dernières années. On peut même dire que parmi toutes les capitales européennes, Berlin possède un caractère unique et son charme provient autant de l'effervescence qui la caractérise que des changements constants d'aspect et d'atmosphère dont elle est le théâtre. L'attraction des autres grandes villes européennes réside quant à elle davantage sur l'image concrète et précise qu'en ont ses habitants et les visiteurs qui s'y rendent.

La vie de quartier de Berlin

Berlin est une mégalopole très étendue. Ses 3,5 millions d'habitants vivent répartis sur 900 km^2 (statistiquement, chaque habitant dispose de 32,9 m^2). C'est sans doute pour cette raison que la vie de quartier a toujours été intense. Beaucoup de Berlinois limitent leur vie sociale et professionnelle à un périmètre déterminé autour de leur domicile, puisque le café préféré est à coté de chez soi, le bar de toujours au coin de la rue et que chaque quartier dispose d'une bonne infrastructure de centres commerciaux et de petits commerces.

Les quartiers

Berlin compte au total 23 quartiers. Cette ouvrage parcourt des résidences situées principalement en centre ville. Nous nous attachons par la suite à décrire les quartiers qui composent le centre.

Charlottenburg

Ce quartier, de nos jours relativement bourgeois et nanti, a connu un essor dans les années 80 grâce aux premiers squatters qui attirèrent l'attention sur lui. En peu de temps des investissements s'effectuèrent sur les anciens bâtiments à moitié effondrés ou en ruines, et les loyers commencèrent à augmenter. A l'époque du Mur, ce quartier était le cœur de Berlin Ouest et la fameuse Kurfürstendamm ainsi que les bars et les clubs nocturnes étaient très a la mode. Aujourd'hui, on se souvient avec une certaine nostalgie de ces temps où il n'était pas nécessaire de surenchérir avec autant de nouvelles attractions. Bien que le Théâtre de l'Ouest et le Palais de Charlottenburg continuent d'être des attractions touristiques importantes, la vie nocturne s'est tournée vers les quartiers de Mitte et de Prenzlauer Berg.

Mitte

Dans les années 20, le quartier de Mitte était le centre culturel de la ville. La construction du Mur et la scission de l'Allemagne le convertirent pendant des années en une zone frontière inaccessible entre Berlin Ouest et Berlin Est. Après la chute du Mur, ce « noman's-land » offrit un immense potentiel en terme de superficie et attira de gros investisseurs ainsi que des architectes renommés et des designers intéressés par la réalisation de projets de construction d'envergure. Au cours de ces dernières années, Mitte est redevenu le centre névralgique de la ville et pendant un certain temps on a pu admirer ici le principal chantier d'Europe. Le paysage urbain du quartier était alors caractérisé par des centaines de grues et d'édifices en construction. Le complexe Sony Center du célèbre architecte Helmut Jahn et l'édifice Debishaus, réalisé par Renzo Piano et qui abrite le siège de Daimler Chrysler, sont quelques-uns des nouveaux symboles de la ville. Les alentours de la rue Auguststraße et des cours Sofia et Heckmann ont vu apparaître une zone dédiée à l'art près des galeries et des points de rencontres culturels. Quant au projet d'urbanisation de la Place de Paris, il a permis de sortir la Porte de Brandebourg (désormais réouverte au trafic) de l'isolement dans lequel son statut de zone frontière l'avait plongée.

Prenzlauer Berg

Le quartier de Berlin Est Prenzlauer Berg était déjà au temps de la République un quartier d'intellectuels et d'artistes. Après la chute du Mur, les adeptes de la scène expérimentale s'y installèrent également. Les nombreux immeubles, caves et locaux vides furent occupés sans plus attendre et transformés en logements, bars ou autres types d'établissements. Ces bâtiments offraient d'extraordinaires possibilités pour la réalisation de projets peu conventionnels. Aujourd'hui, ce quartier traditionnellement ouvrier s'est converti en une zone très appréciée pour vivre et sortir le soir; en témoignent ses cafés florissants, ses bars et ses galeries.

Schöneberg

Le quartier de Schöneberg, avec ses petites boutiques, son ambiance décadente et agréable ainsi que le charme de ses grands édifices anciens, est depuis toujours une zone très appréciée pour vivre. De plus, les nombreux cafés, bars et restaurants créent une atmosphère animée de jour comme de nuit.

Kreuzberg

Le quartier de Kreuzberg, où durant des années les squatters et la scène alternative attiraient l'attention du public, est devenu aujourd'hui plus tranquille. Auparavant, la partie est de Kreuzberg était connue sous le nom de « Quartier SO 36 » (SO de par sa situation géographique et 36 pour les derniers numéros du code postal). C'est à cet endroit que le métro arrivait à son terminus, puisque la dernière station correspondait

à la limite avec le Mur. Aujourd'hui, Kreuzberg est un quartier haut en couleur et riche de la culture que les grandes communautés turques installées depuis de nombreuses générations lui apportent. Sa situation centrale, les nombreux bâtiments anciens et la vie nocturne toujours animée maintiennent l'intérêt pour de nouveaux projets d'investissement.

Friedrichshain

Treize ans après la chute du Mur, le vieux quartier ouvrier de Friedrichshain est devenu le refuge de tous ceux qui ont fui les zones de Mitte et Prenzlauer Berg, devenues trop chères à cause des réformes et des travaux de construction aux coûts exorbitants. La Spree sépare Friedrichshain de Kreuzberg et la seule liaison entre les deux quartiers est le pont d'Oberbaum. Les loyers sont encore accessibles et offrent un terrain et un espace idéaux pour l'apparition d'une nouvelle sous-culture.

Zehlendorf

Zehlendorf se trouve au sud ouest de la ville, à l'écart du centre, en pleine campagne. Entouré de bois, de parcs et de nombreux lacs, il est proche des espaces verts de la ville, Wannsee et Grunewald. Dans ce quartier privilégié se sont installés principalement une classe nantie et l'élite des milieux d'architectes et de design, qui se reposent de l'agitation de la ville dans d'élégantes maisons individuelles ou dans de nobles demeures.

L'impulsion de la ville

Suite à la chute du Mur et au redémarrage économique des anciens quartiers de l'Est, la ville a connu de nombreuses mutations. Les quartiers animés attirent principalement l'attention des jeunes et des nouveaux arrivants. Cependant, depuis toujours la riche sous-culture berlinoise joue le rôle d'indicateur des quartiers à la mode. Comme au jeu du chat et de la souris, les zones les plus populaires et les plus sollicitées se calquent toujours sur celles où le mouvement culturel et artistique alternatif est le plus vivace. Les investisseurs ont donc toujours suivi la piste de ces nouveaux quartiers à la mode. Mais dès que commençaient les travaux de rénovation et d'embellissement de la zone, le mouvement culturel partait dans d'autres quartiers, en quête de nouveaux espaces vierges.

Qu'est ce qui fait de Berlin une ville si attirante?

En réalité, Berlin n'est pas une ville cosmopolite. Malgré la fièvre métropolitaine qui s'est emparé d'elle après la chute du Mur, la ville a gardé un caractère propre très marqué. Sous beaucoup d'aspects elle est presque provinciale, bien qu'elle ait toujours été le théâtre d'événements politiques et culturels importants. Les légendaires années 20, les cabarets nocturnes et les spectacles de revue très en vogue à l'époque, forment désormais partie de l'histoire pour toujours. Beaucoup d'architectes, d'artistes et de scientifiques célèbres tels que Walter Gropius, Hans Scharoun, Bruno Taut, Emil Fahrenkamp, Hans Pelzig, Martin Wagner, Max Liebermann, Max Beckmann, Bertolt Brecht, Arnold Zweig et Kurt Tucholsky ont laissé leur emprunte dans la ville. La scission de l'Allemagne, qui l'a presque transformée en île, a en fait renforcé le caractère de la ville et de ses habitants. D'autre part, en plus de l'offre culturelle quasi illimitée, les nombreux parcs, situés aussi bien dans le centre qu'en périphérie offrent une grande qualité de vie. Sur quasiment un quart de la superficie totale de Berlin, on trouve des bois, des lacs et des fleuves qui offrent un espace de détente, mais aussi la possibilité de pratiquer des loisirs de plein air. Au centre ville, le lieu de promenade préféré des Berlinois est le Tiergarten, un parc boisé qui en été, devient le lieu idéal pour un barbecue.

L'histoire récente de la ville

Historiquement, la ville de Berlin a vécu des époques de gloire. Mais elle a également connu des moments de profonde décadence. Les conséquences de la deuxième guerre mondiale ont un impact indéniable sur son histoire récente. Rappelons que la ville avait été réduite à un tas de décombres. Plus de 600.000 logements (1 immeuble sur 3) furent détruits. Grâce à l'effort suprême réalisé par les dénommées « femmes des ruines », un grand nombre d'édifices construits pendant la période du « Gründerzeit » ou « années de spéculation » (1870-1900) ont pu être conservés. Plus tard, la construction du Mur imposa à la ville des années de division douloureuse. Le 9 novembre 1989, lorsque les frontières s'ouvrirent à nouveau, la ville présentait deux visages bien différents. Après la seconde guerre mondiale, la dévastation qu'avait subi Berlin Ouest tout comme Berlin Est, était d'une ampleur telle que la reconstruction était urgente. Cependant, dans la partie est de la ville, sous le contrôle communiste, le projet de reconstruction était basé sur un critère quantitatif et donna lieu á l'édification des « Plattenbausiedlungen », ces énormes blocs uniformes préfabriqués qui dominaient le paysage architectural. Dans la partie Ouest en revanche, les projets étaient coordonnés dans le but d'assainir le cœur de la ville et les édifices érigés répondaient au principe de qualité de vie.

La chute du Mur engendra une période de changements constants et illimités. La ville attira des personnes du monde entier désireuses de participer à ces moments d'euphorie et de métamorphose. La décision de rendre à Berlin son statut de capitale et de métropole plongea la ville pendant des années dans une fièvre de planification et de reconstruction. Treize ans après la chute du Mur, le pouls de Berlin a retrouvé un rythme tranquille et l'équilibre s'installe. Cependant, dans beaucoup de domaines, la réunification allemande ne s'est pas totalement accomplie et il reste encore beaucoup d'idées et de projets à concrétiser. La ville de Berlin semble donc avoir encore un bel avenir devant elle.

Ce livre veut donner une vision variée de la culture urbaine de Berlin. Il montre des maisons particulières, réhabilitées et décorées par des architectes et des designers de renom : Stefan Sterf, Heinz Hellermann, Barkow Leibinger, ou encore par des cabinets d'architecture prestigieux : Grollwitz Zappe, Peanutz, Hoyer & Schindele. Cet ouvrage montre également des maisons rénovées grâce à l'effort et à l'initiative des ses propriétaires, avec des moyens économiques limités; ce qui reflète à la perfection l'esprit berlinois. Le caractère dynamique et bigarré dc cette ville se manifeste à travers un large éventail de possibilités en terme d'espaces et de formes de vie. Cela va des lofts et des appartements minimalistes dotés des dernières avancées technologiques, aux immeubles d'artistes à l'atmosphère unique et particulière, en passant par d'anciennes résidences seigneuriales datant de la fin du XIXe siècle, ou encore des maisons individuelles dans des zones vertes de la banlieue, où leurs habitants fuient l'agitation du centre.

Introducción

Probablemente, ninguna otra ciudad de Europa haya experimentado en las últimas décadas una metamorfosis tan espectacular como Berlín. Podría decirse que, entre todas las metrópolis y capitales europeas, Berlín tiene un carácter especial y que su encanto reside tanto en la viva actividad que la caracteriza como en los constantes cambios de aspecto y ambiente que vive. Por el contrario, el atractivo de otras grandes ciudades europeas se basa más bien en la imagen concreta y determinada que tienen sus habitantes y los visitantes que a ellas acuden.

La vida de barrio de Berlín

Berlín es una ciudad grande, sobre todo en extensión. Sus 3,5 millones de habitantes viven repartidos en 900 km^2 (estadísticamente hablando, cada habitante dispone de 32,9 m^2). Probablemente sea éste el motivo principal por el que, desde siempre, se ha desarrollado una intensiva vida de barrio. Muchos berlineses limitan su vida social y profesional a un determinado radio alrededor de su domicilio, ya que el café preferido está al lado de casa, el bar de toda la vida en la esquina y en todos los barrios existe una buena infraestructura de centros comerciales y pequeños establecimientos.

Los barrios

En total hay 23 barrios. En este libro aparecen viviendas situadas, sobre todo, en el centro de la ciudad. A continuación se describen las zonas más céntricas.

Charlottenburg

Este barrio, actualmente de carácter más bien burgués y pudiente, comenzó a vivir un auge en los años ochenta, cuando los primeros okupas despertaron la atención sobre él. De pronto se empezó a invertir dinero en los antiguos edificios, medio desmoronados y en ruinas, y al poco tiempo empezaron a subir los alquileres. En tiempos del Muro, este barrio era además el núcleo central de Berlín Oeste y la famosa Kurfürstendamm y los bares y locales nocturnos que allí había se pusieron de moda. Hoy en día, en el barrio se recuerdan con cierta nostalgia aquellos tiempos en los que no había que competir con tantas nuevas atracciones. Aunque el Teatro del Oeste y el Palacio de Charlottenburg siguen siendo destinos turísticos principales, la vida nocturna se ha trasladado a los barrios de Mitte y Prenzlauer Berg.

Mitte

En la década de 1920, el barrio de Mitte era el centro cultural de la ciudad. La construcción del Muro y la escisión de Alemania lo convirtieron durante décadas en una zona fronteriza e inaccesible entre Berlín Oriental y Berlín Occidental. Tras la caída del Muro, esta desaprovechada franja de tierra de nadie ofrecía un inmenso potencial de superficie y atrajo a grandes inversores, a famosos arquitectos y diseñadores interesados en llevar a cabo interesantes proyectos de construcción. Durante los últimos años, este barrio se ha convertido de nuevo en el centro neurálgico de la ciudad y durante varios años pudo admirarse aquí la mayor obra de Europa. El paisaje de las calles del barrio lo configuraban cientos de grúas y de edificios en construcción. Algunos de los destacados nuevos "símbolos" de la ciudad son el complejo Sony Center del famoso arquitecto Helmut Jahn y el edificio Debishaus, sede

Daimler Chrysler, realizado por Renzo Piano. Alrededor de la calle Auguststraße y de los patios Sofía y Heckmann ha surgido una zona dedicada al arte con galerías y puntos de encuentro culturales. El proyecto de reurbanización de la plaza de París ha liberado la Puerta de Brandeburgo, de nuevo abierta al tráfico, del aislamiento en que la había sumido su carácter de zona fronteriza.

Prenzlauer Berg
Ya en tiempos de la República Democrática Alemana, el distrito de Berlín Oriental Prenzlauer Berg era un barrio de intelectuales y artistas. Tras la caída del Muro se mudaron también a este barrio adeptos a la escena experimental. Los numerosos pisos, sótanos y locales vacíos fueron ocupados sin más y acondicionados como viviendas, bares u otro tipo de establecimientos. Estos edificios ofrecían extraordinarias posibilidades de hacer realidad ideas poco convencionales. Hoy, este barrio tradicionalmente obrero se ha convertido, con sus florecientes cafés, bares y galerías en una zona muy apreciada para vivir y salir por la noche.

Schöneberg
El barrio de Schöneberg, con sus pequeñas tiendas, su característico y atractivo ambiente algo decadente y el encanto de los grandes edificios antiguos ha sido desde siempre un zona muy apreciada para vivir. Además, los numerosos cafés, bares y restaurantes le dan ambiente y mucha vida, de día y de noche.

Kreuzberg
El barrio de Kreuzberg, donde durante décadas los okupas y la escena alternativa atraían la atención pública, se ha vuelto algo más tranquilo. Antaño, la parte oriental de Kreuzberg era conocida como "Barrio SO 36" (SO por su situación geográfica al sureste y 36 por los números finales del código postal), en el que el metro llegaba a su fin porque la última estación era a la vez el límite con el Muro. Hoy en día, Kreuzberg se caracteriza por el movimiento y el colorido que le dan las grandes comunidades turcas asentadas allí desde hace muchas generaciones. Su céntrica situación, los numerosos edificios antiguos y la todavía importante vida nocturna hacen que este barrio siga resultando interesante para nuevos proyectos de inversión.

Friedrichshain
Trece años después de la caída del Muro, el antiguo barrio obrero de Friedrichshain se ha convertido, sobre todo, en refugio de todos aquellos que huyeron de las zonas de Mitte y Prenzlauer Berg porque éstas se habían encarecido demasiado a causa de las reformas y de las obras de construcción millonarias. El río Spree lo separa del barrio de Kreuzberg y su única vía de comunicación es el puente de Oberbaum. Los alquileres son todavía asequibles y ofrecen el substrato y el espacio ideales para la aparición de una nueva subcultura.

Zehlendorf

Zehlendorf está al suroeste de la ciudad, algo alejado del centro, en pleno campo, junto a las zonas verdes de esparcimiento de la ciudad, Wannsee y Grunewald, rodeado de bosques, parques y numerosos lagos. En este privilegiado barrio se han establecido principalmente una clase adinerada y la elite de la arquitectura y el diseño, que descansan del ajetreo de la ciudad en elegantes casas unifamiliares o nobles mansiones.

El impulso de la ciudad

Con la caída del Muro y la reactivación de la vida económica de los antiguos barrios del este, la ciudad ha experimentado muchos cambios. Los barrios con más vida y movimiento son los que llaman la atención principalmente a la gente joven y a los recién llegados. Sin embargo, desde siempre, la rica subcultura berlinesa ha sido responsable en gran medida de marcar los barrios de moda. Como en el juego del ratón y el gato, las zonas más populares y solicitadas cambiaban de lugar y reaparecían allí donde renacía en ese momento el ambiente cultural y artístico experimental y alternativo. Los inversores seguían la pista de estos nuevos barrios de moda y tan pronto como empezaban los trabajos de renovación y embellecimiento de la zona, el foco cultural se hacía a la búsqueda de nuevos rincones en otros barrios.

¿Qué hace de Berlín una ciudad tan atractiva?

En realidad, Berlín no es una ciudad cosmopolita. A pesar de la fiebre metropolitana que surgió tras la caída del Muro, la ciudad ha mantenido un carácter propio muy marcado. En muchos aspectos resulta casi provinciana y, sin embargo, siempre ha sido un lugar de gran actividad política y cultural. Los legendarios años veinte y los cabarets nocturnos y espectáculos de revista que tan en boga estaban en aquella época han pasado a formar parte para siempre a la historia. Muchos arquitectos, artistas y científicos famosos como Walter Gropius, Hans Scharoun, Bruno Taut, Emil Fahrenkamp, Hans Pelzig, Martin Wagner, Max Liebermann, Max Beckmann, Bertolt Brecht, Arnold Zweig y Kurt Tucholsky, entre otros, dejaron su huella en la ciudad. Durante la escisión de Alemania, su especial situación geográfica como "isla" fortaleció todavía más el carácter de la ciudad y de sus habitantes. Además de la casi ilimitada oferta cultural, también los numerosos parques, tanto en el centro como en los alrededores, ofrecen una gran calidad de vida. Casi una cuarta parte de la superficie total de Berlín está cubierta por bosques, lagos y ríos que procuran descanso y muchas posibilidades de practicar actividades de ocio al aire libre. En el centro de la ciudad, el lugar de descanso preferido es el Tiergarten, un parque poblado de árboles que en verano se convierte en el sitio ideal para hacer una barbacoa.

Historia reciente de la ciudad

Históricamente, la ciudad de Berlín ha tenido épocas de gloria pero también muchos momentos de profunda decadencia. Las consecuencias de la Segunda Guerra Mundial influyeron directamente en su historia más reciente. Por una parte, la ciudad quedó reducida a un montón de escombros. Fueron destruidas más de 600.000 viviendas (un edificio de cada tres). Gracias al impresionante esfuerzo realizado por las llamadas "mujeres de las ruinas" se logró conservar un gran número de edificios construidos durante el llamado Gründerzeit o años de la especulación (1870-1900). Posteriormente, el levantamiento del Muro impuso a la ciudad décadas de dolorosa división. El 9 de noviembre de 1989, cuando se abrieron de nuevo las fronteras, la ciudad presentaba dos caras bien diferentes. Tras la Segunda Guerra Mundial, la devastación que habían sufrido tanto Berlín Oriental como Berlín Occidental era de tal magnitud, que la reconstrucción se hacía urgente. Sin embargo, mientras en la parte este de la ciudad, bajo mando comunista, el proyecto de reconstrucción de edificios se basó en la cantidad y en las llamadas *plattenbausiedlungen* o uniformes y enormes bloques prefabricados que dominaban el paisaje arquitectónico, en Berlín Oeste se llevaron a cabo proyectos de saneamiento del núcleo urbano y se levantaron nuevos edificios atendiendo, sobre todo, al principio de calidad.

La caída del Muro dio paso a una época de cambios continuos e ilimitados. La ciudad atrajo a gentes de todas partes del mundo que querían participar de aquellos momentos de euforia y metamorfosis. La decisión de devolver a Berlín su condición de capital y metrópoli hizo que la ciudad viviera sumida durante años en una fiebre de planificación y reconstrucción. Trece años después de la caída del Muro, el pulso de Berlín se ha vuelto algo más tranquilo y se empieza a hacer balance. Sin embargo, en muchos campos la reunificación de Alemania no se ha consumado totalmente y quedan aún muchas ideas y posibilidades que realizar. Así, se puede afirmar que la ciudad tiene todavía un interesante futuro ante sí.

Este libro quiere dar una visión de la variada cultura urbana de Berlín. En él se muestran domicilios particulares rehabilitados y decorados por arquitectos y diseñadores individuales de renombre –Stefan Sterf, Heinz Hellermann, Barkow-Leibinger– o por prestigiosos despachos de arquitectos –como Grollwitz Zappe, Peanutz, Hoyer & Schindele, entre otros–, pero también viviendas reformadas desde el esfuerzo y la iniciativa de sus dueños con medios económicos limitados, lo que refleja a la perfección el espíritu berlinés. El carácter dinámico y variopinto de esta ciudad se manifiesta en el ámbito de las formas de vida y espacio privados en un amplio abanico de posibilidades que abarca desde lofts y pisos minimalistas dotados de los últimos avances tecnológicos hasta viviendas de artistas con un ambiente propio y particular, pasando por antiguos pisos señoriales de finales del siglo XIX o casas unifamiliares en zonas ajardinadas de las afueras, donde sus habitantes se refugian del bullicio del centro.

Der L-förmige Grundriss dieser Wohnung gruppiert sich um das sogenannte „Berliner Zimmer" – ein Zimmer, welches an der inneren Gebäudeecke liegt und nur vom Hof belichtet wird. In dieser Wohnung wird es als Esszimmer genutzt. Ursprünglich lagen die Gesellschaftsräume zur Straße, während Kinderzimmer und Bedienstetenräume zum Hof orientiert waren. Beim Umbau der Wohnung stand die Neupositionierung der Räume und die Auflösung der zellenartigen Raumaufteilung für eine Anpassung an moderne Wohnanforderungen im Vordergrund. Im Flur wurde eine Wand aus Stahl, durchscheinendem Glas und Birkenholz eingebaut und bildet mit den Schiebetüren der Schlafräume ein integrales System.

The L shape of this home is centered round a so-called Berliner room – a room situated in an interior corner of the building that only receives light from the courtyard. It is now used as a dining room. In the old days, the less private spaces faced the street while the children's and servants' bedrooms overlooked the courtyard. The priorities of the conversion were the reorientation of the rooms and the rearrangement of the enclosed compartments to adapt them to modern domestic needs. A wall made of steel, translucent glass and birch was put up in the corridor, combining with the bedrooms' sliding doors to form an integral system.

L'étage en forme de L de cette maison s'organise autour de la pièce appelée « la chambre berlinoise », qui se trouve dans le coin intérieur de l'édifice et qui reçoit uniquement la lumière du patio. Dans cette maison, la pièce sert de salle à manger. Auparavant, les espaces les moins intimes donnaient sur la rue, tandis que les chambres des enfants et les salles d'eau donnaient sur les cours intérieures. Durant les travaux, on a donné priorité à la réorientation des pièces ainsi qu'à une distribution adaptée aux nécessités domestiques. On a bâti dans le couloir un mur en acier, en verre translucide et bois de bouleau, qui forme avec les portes coulissantes des chambres un système complet.

La planta en forma de L de esta vivienda se agrupa en torno a la llamada "habitación berlinesa", una estancia situada en una esquina interior del edificio que sólo recibe luz a través del patio. En esta vivienda la habitación se utiliza como comedor. Antaño, los espacios menos íntimos se orientaban hacia la calle, mientras que las habitaciones de los niños y de servicio daban a los patios. En la reforma de la casa, la reorientación de las estancias y el abono de una distribución de compartimentos estanco de las habitaciones para adaptarlas a las necesidades domésticas modernas fueron una prioridad. En el pasillo se levantó una pared de acero, cristal translúcido y abedul que junto con las puertas correderas de los dormitorios forma un sistema integral.

Location: **Charlottenburg**
Architect: **Barkow-Leibinger**
Photos: **© Werner Huthmacher**

Berliner room

Barkow-Leibinger

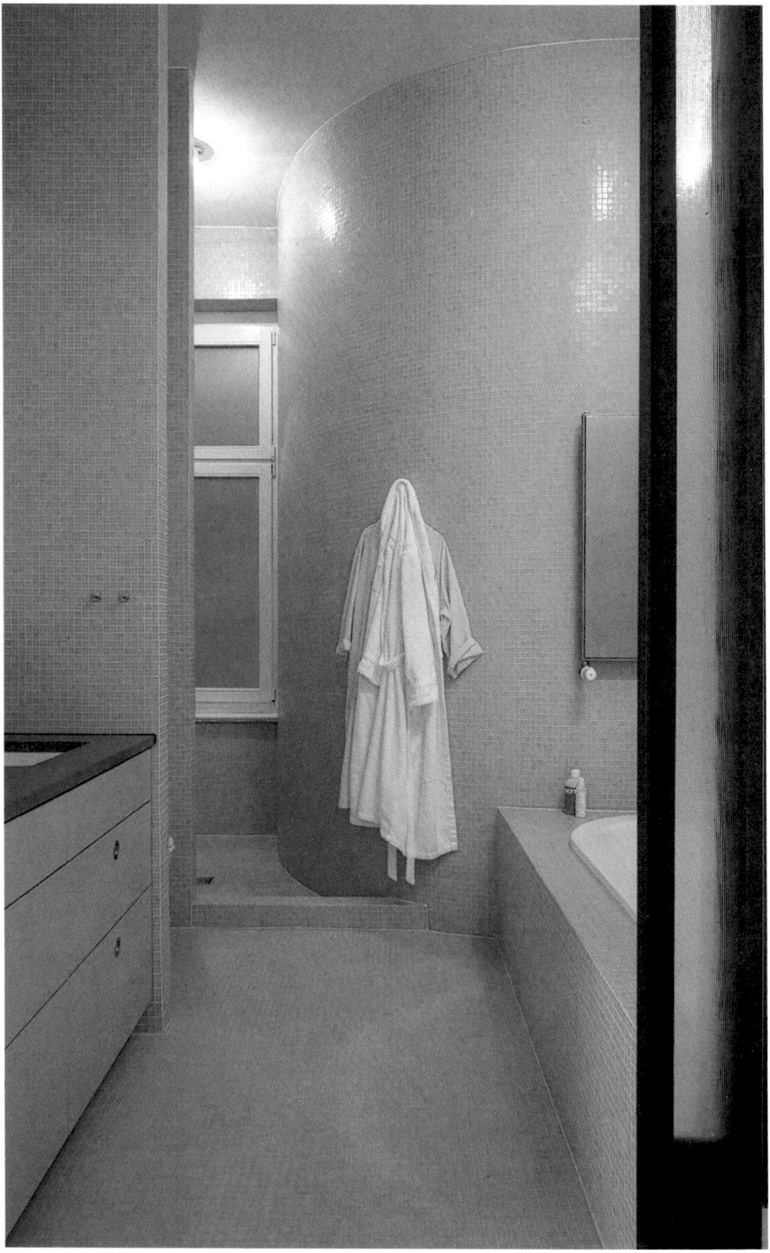

In dieser 240 m² großen Altbauwohnung im Stadtteil Charlottenburg wohnt und arbeitet das Architektenehepaar Natascha und Philipp Meuser mit ihrem vierjährigen Sohn Paul. Kommt man zur Haustür herein und lässt den Blick bis zum Ende der Wohnung durch die geöffneten Flügeltüren bis ins Schlafzimmers schweifen, so erscheint einem die Strecke ewig. Die ineinander fließenden Zimmer mit den 3,65 Meter hohen Decken bieten Licht, Sicht und Raum. Möbel und Accessoires wurden gekonnt kombiniert und stellen eine Mischung aus Biedermeier, Barock, verschiedenen Objekten aus den 30er Jahren und modernem praktischen Mobiliar dar.

This old 2,600 square foot apartment in the Charlottenburg neighborhood is where the architects Natascha and Philipp Meuser work and live with their four-year old son Paul. From the main entrance the eye is led, seemingly to infinity, through paneled doors until it reaches the bedroom at the rear of the home. The inner rooms, which lead onto each other, are endowed with light, views and a spaciousness that is enhanced by the 12 foot high ceilings. The furnishings are shrewdly put together in a mixture of the Biedermeier and Baroque styles, with functional furniture and various objects from the 1930s.

Le couple d'architectes Natascha et Philipp Meuser ainsi que leur fils de quatre ans, Paul, habitent et travaillent dans ce vieil appartement de 240 m² du quartier de Charlottenburg. Depuis l'entrée principale, le regard se fraie un chemin entre les portes battantes pour arriver jusqu'à la chambre, située au fond de la maison. Les pièces intérieures, en enfilade, offrent grâce à leur 3,65 m de hauteur, lumière, perspective et ampleur. Les meubles et les accessoires ont été réunis avec goût. On retrouve le sytle Biedermeier et le style baroque à travers différents objets des années 30 et des meubles fonctionnels.

En este piso antiguo de 240 m² del barrio de Charlottenburg vive y trabaja la pareja de arquitectos Natascha y Philipp Meuser con su hijo de cuatro años, Paul. Desde la entrada principal, la mirada se abre paso entre puertas de batientes hasta llegar al dormitorio del fondo de la casa, en un recorrido que deviene eterno. Las habitaciones interiores, que conducen de una a otra, ofrecen con sus 3,65 m de altura luz, perspectiva y amplitud. Los muebles y accesorios están combinados con sabiduría y constituyen una mezcla de los estilos Biedermeier y Barroco, con diferentes objetos de los años 30 y piezas de mobiliario funcional.

Location: **Charlottenburg**
Architect: **The Meusers**
Photos: **© Mad Mogensen**

Old apartment

The Meusers

In dieser Wohnung gibt es fünf Bücherzimmer, in denen sich in riesigen, zum großen Teil selbst gezimmerten Regalen, fast vierzigtausend gedruckte Werke türmen. Zwei kleine Wohnungen wurden verbunden, um Raum für Wohn- und Stauplatz zu schaffen. Auf Tischen liegen Bücher zum Anschauen und Lesen bereit und die überall an den Wänden hängenden Kunstwerke laden zum Betrachten ein. Das Deckengemälde im größten Bücherzimmer ist vom englischen Künstler Burt Irvin. Verpönt ist in dieser Wohnung modernes High Tech und vergebens hält man Ausschau nach Kommunikationsmitteln wie Fernseher und Radio.

There are five rooms given over to books in this home: almost 40,000 volumes are stacked in huge bookcases, some of them built by the resident himself. He only found enough space to store so many books and also have a living area for himself by joining up two apartments. Some books lie on the tables, waiting to be perused, while the paintings dotting the walls also invite contemplation. The fresco adorning the ceiling of the main library is by the English artist Burt Irvin. Modern technology is not welcome here and visitors will search in vain for a television or radio.

Cinq pièces sont consacrées dans cette maison à la bibliothèque. Sur d'énormes étagères, certaines construites par le propriétaire lui-même, sont entreposés plus de 40.000 livres. C'est seulement en réunissant deux appartements qu'on a pu trouver l'espace nécessaire pour à la fois vivre et garder autant de livres. Certains exemplaires sont posés sur les tables en attendant d'être feuilletés. Tout comme les peintures qui recouvrent la totalité des murs nous invitent à la contemplation. La fresque qui décore le plafond de la bibliothèque principale a été réalisée par l'artiste anglais Burt Irvin. Dans cette maison les nouvelles technologies sont mal vues, et c'est en vain que l'on cherche la télévision ou la radio.

En esta casa hay cinco habitaciones dedicadas a biblioteca. En enormes librerías, algunas construidas por el residente mismo, se apilan casi 40.000 volúmenes. Sólo uniendo dos viviendas se obtuvo el espacio suficiente para vivir y almacenar tantos libros. Algunos ejemplares descansan sobre las mesas esperando ser hojeados. Las pinturas que recubren las paredes por doquier nos invitan a su contemplación. El fresco que adorna el techo de la biblioteca principal es del artista inglés Burt Irvin. La tecnología moderna está aquí mal vista y en vano busca uno aparatos como la televisión o la radio.

By the resident

Beim Umbau wurde der Zuschnitt dieser 150 m² großen Gründerzeitwohnung an moderne Wohnbedürfnisse angepasst. Die modernen, neuen Einbauten bilden einen reizvollen Kontrast zu dem alten Baubestand, von dem vor allem die hohen Stuckdecken und verschiedenen Parkettböden erhalten wurden. Einige Wohnfunktionen wurden umgelegt oder großzügig geöffnet. Die ehemalige Küche ist jetzt ein modernes und funktionelles Badezimmer. In der neuen Küche befinden sich drei freistehende Kuben, von denen der Schrank und die Anrichte als Raumteiler dienen, während man vom Kochblock aus die Aussicht nach draußen genießen kann.

The conversion of this 1,600 square-foot Gründerzeit-style apartment adapted it to the requirements of a modern home. The new architectural additions provide a delightful, stimulating contrast with the old structure, which is particularly prominent in the high stucco ceilings and the various parquet floors. Some spaces were rearranged or generously opened up. So, the former kitchen is now a modern functional bathroom. Three free-standing cubes have been inserted. Two of these – the closet and the dresser – serve to mark off spaces, while the block in the kitchen provides the chance to enjoy the view outside.

Durant les travaux, le réaménagement de cet appartement de 150 m² de style Gründerzeit s'est adapté aux nécessités d'un logement moderne. Les ajouts architecturaux contrastent fortement avec l'ancienne structure qui continue d'exister à travers les hauts plafonds en stuc et les différents parquets. Certains espaces de la maison ont été disposés d'une autre façon et sont très ouverts. Ainsi l'ancienne cuisine est aujourd'hui une salle de bain moderne et fonctionnelle. On y trouve trois cubes placés librement. Deux d'entre eux, l'armoire et le buffet, servent à séparer les espaces, tandis que depuis le bloc cuisine on peut profiter de la vue extérieure.

En la reforma, el corte de este piso de 150 m² estilo Gründerzeit se adaptó a las necesidades de una vivienda moderna. Los nuevos añadidos arquitectónicos constituyen un estimulante y encantador contraste a la estructura antigua, que pervive especialmente en los altos techos estucados y en los diferentes suelos de parquet. Algunos espacios de la vivienda se dispusieron de otro modo o se abrieron generosamente. Así, la antigua cocina es ahora una cuarto de baño moderno y funcional. En ella hay tres cubos colocados libremente. Dos de ellos, el armario y el aparador, sirven de separación entre espacios, mientras que desde el bloque de la cocina se puede disfrutar de las vistas al exterior.

Location: **Charlottenburg**
Architect: **Hüfer Ramin**
Photos: **© Werner Huthmacher**

Hüfer Ramin

In diesem Loft hat man versucht, einen harmonischen Einklang zwischen alter Baustruktur und neuen, modernen Elementen zu schaffen. Das alte Ziegelmauerwerk wurde freigelegt und zum großen Teil erhalten, der Schornsteinblock musste aus statischen Gründen versetzt werden. Der riesige Wintergarten mit einer Deckenhöhe von 5,90 Metern schafft ausreichend Licht und das Glasdach lässt sich öffnen. Auch im Badezimmer mit Naturschieferkacheln fehlt es durch die mit Fenstern versehene Dachkonstruktion nicht an Licht und man hat zudem einen schönen Blick zur Dachterrasse. In der Küche dominiert die raummittig eingebaute Kochstelle.

This loft sought a harmony between the structure of the original building and the modern additions. Most of the brick walls have not only been retained but also left exposed, although the fireplace had to be moved to comply with building regulations. The enormous conservatory (almost 20 ft/6 m tall) provides enough light and the glass roof opens onto the outside world. Similarly, there is no lack of light in the bathroom – clad with natural slate tiles – thanks to the skylights in the ceiling; it also offers a beautiful view of the roof terrace. In the kitchen, the main attraction is undoubtedly the cooking unit placed in the center.

On a voulu atteindre dans ce loft une certaine harmonie entre la structure de la construction originelle et les nouveaux éléments. Lors de la réforme le mur en briques apparentes a été conservé dans sa plus grande partie, si bien qu'on a dû déplacer la cheminée pour des raisons statiques. L'énorme serre qui fait 5,90 m de hauteur et qui a un toit en verre ouvrant, fait entrer la lumière en abondance. La salle de bain, dont le sol est recouvert de carrelage en ardoise naturelle, est elle aussi très bien éclairée grâce aux lucarnes supérieures, et offre une superbe vue sur la terrasse. Dans la cuisine, le principal élément est biensûr la cuisinière, qui a été installée au milieu de la pièce.

En este loft se pretendió lograr la armonía entre la estructura de la vieja construcción y los nuevos elementos modernos. El muro de ladrillo se dejó a la vista en bastantes espacios, si bien la chimenea tuvo que trasladarse por motivos estáticos. El enorme invernadero, con una altura de 5,90 metros aporta luz suficiente y el techo de cristal se abre al exterior. Tampoco falta luz en el baño, recubierto por baldosas de pizarra natural, gracias a las claraboyas superiores. Desde él se puede disfrutar además de una preciosa vista sobre la azotea. En la cocina, los protagonistas son los fogones, colocados en el centro.

64

In diesem 220 m² großen Altbau dominiert die Kunst in fast allen Teilen der Wohnung. Die Mischung verschiedener Stilrichtungen erweckt zugleich einen Eindruck von Eleganz, Gemütlichkeit und Farbenreichtum. Einige alte Möbel stammen aus dem Familienschloss der Hausherrin, die meisten Objekte sind jedoch Errungenschaften vom Sammlermarkt. Das große Esszimmer ist gleichzeitig auch Arbeits- und Besprechungszimmer und im puristischen Stil eingerichtet. Ein graues minimalistisches Werk des Engländers Alan Charlton und der lange schwere Eichentisch dominieren den Raum. Der lange Korridor, der zu Herrn Oroschakoffs Arbeitsraum führt, wird von Werken junger moderner Künstler geschmückt.

Art is everywhere in this aristocratic, 2,340-square foot apartment. The mixture of various styles gives the sensation of elegance, comfort and chromatic richness in equal measure. Some of the antique furniture came from the owner's family castle, but most of the objects were bought in art galleries. The enormous dining room, decorated in a purist style, serves as both an office and a meeting room. A minimalist gray-colored painting by the English artist Alan Charlton and a large solid-oak table dominate the sitting room. The long corridor leading to Herr Oroschakoff's office is decorated with works by young contemporary artists.

Dans cet appartement seigneurial de 220 m², l'art est omniprésent. Le mélange des styles procure une sensation d'élégance, de confort et de richesse chromatique. Quelques meubles anciens proviennent du château de famille de Madame la propriétaire, mais la majeure partie des objets vient du marché de l'art. L'immense salle à manger décorée dans un style puriste, fait à la fois office de bureau et de salle de réunion. Une œuvre de l'Anglais Alan Charlton, grise et minimaliste, ainsi qu'une longue table en chêne massif dominent la salle. Le long couloir qui mène au bureau de Monsieur Oroschakoff est décoré avec des œuvres de jeunes artistes contemporains.

En este piso señorial de 220 m², el arte es algo omnipresente. La mezcla de estilos diversos proporciona por igual una sensación de elegancia, confort y riqueza cromática. Algunos muebles antiguos pertenecían al castillo de la familia de la dueña de la casa, pero la mayor parte de los objetos provienen del mercado del arte. El enorme comedor, decorado en un estilo purista, es a un tiempo despacho y sala de reuniones. Una obra minimalista en color gris del inglés Alan Charlton y la larga mesa de roble macizo dominan la sala. El largo pasillo que lleva al despacho del señor Oroschakoff está decorado con obras de jóvenes artistas modernos.

Location: **Charlottenburg**
Architect: **H. G. Oroschakoff**
and the Countess von
Hohenthal und Bergen
Photos: © **Reto Guntli**

H. G. Oroschakoff and the
Countess von Hohenthal und Bergen

Diese Wohnung befindet sich in einem Jugendstilgebäude aus dem Jahre 1903, das aufgrund seiner geschichtlichen und künstlerischen Bedeutung unter Denkmalschutz steht. 1995 wurde die 242 m² große Wohnung mit 7 Zimmern, Bad, WC, Küche, Diele, Wintergarten und Balkon mit dem Ziel saniert, den Originalzustand der Wohnung weitgehend zu erhalten. Bei der Renovierung wurden die alten Parkettböden repariert und nur in der Diele und den Schlafräumen durch neue Holzböden ersetzt. In der Küche restaurierte man den alten Klinkerfußboden. Badezimmer und WC wurden komplett saniert sowie in der ganzen Wohnung neue Elektro- und Sanitärinstallationen gelegt.

This home is situated in a Jugendstil (Central European Art Nouveau) building dating from 1903, which is a listed monument due to its artistic and historic importance. In 1995 the 2,600-square foot apartment – with seven bedrooms and a bathroom, toilet, kitchen, hall, verandah and balcony – was refurbished with the intention of preserving its original state. Almost all the original parquet floor was repaired, with new floorboards being introduced in only the hall and the bedrooms. The bathroom and toilet were completely overhauled; the electrical and plumbing installations throughout the apartment are also new.

Cette maison se trouve dans un immeuble du Jugendstil (Art Noveau centre européen) datant de 1903, et est un monument classé du fait de sa valeur artistique et historique. En 1995, l'appartement de 242 m² comprenant sept chambres, une salle de bain, des toilettes, une cuisine, un vestibule, un balcon et une verrière, a été réhabilité dans l'idée de conserver l'état originel de la demeure. Durant les travaux, on a rénové presque intégralement le parquet en bois d'origine; seul le sol du le vestibule et des chambres est nouveau, tout comme les installations électriques et sanitaires de l'appartement.

Esta vivienda se encuentra en una finca Jugendstil (modernismo centroeuropeo) de 1903, que a causa de su significado histórico y artístico está catalogada como monumento protegido. En 1995, el piso, de 242 m² y siete habitaciones, baño, servicio, cocina, vestíbulo, invernadero y balcón, fue reformado, pero manteniendo la intención de conservar el estado original de la vivienda. En la reforma se reparó el parquet de madera original casi en su totalidad; solamente se colocó tarima nueva en el vestíbulo y en los dormitorios. El cuarto de baño y el servicio fueron reformados completamente y las instalaciones eléctricas y sanitarias también son nuevas en todo el piso.

Location: **Charlottenburg**
Architect: **H. A. Hellermann**
Photos: **© Werner Huthmacher**

A Jugendstil building

H. A. Hellermann

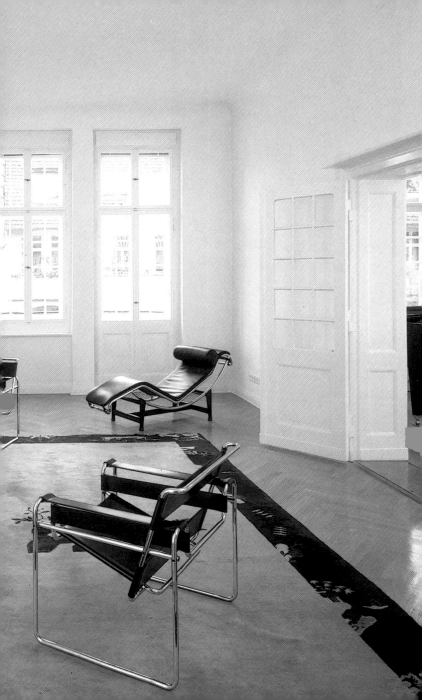

In dieser 125 m² großen, von der Architektin Anna Maske und dem Künstler Fausto Faini bewohnten Altbauwohnung spielen die Gestaltung mit Farbe und die Überschneidung von Kunst und Architektur eine zentrale Rolle. Für ihre Tochter hat Anna Maske eine „architecture en miniature" geschaffen, ein kleines Raumgefüge mit zwei Läden, Straßen- und Hoffassade nach eigenen Entwürfen und von Gio Ponti handbemalt, welches zum Experimentieren und Improvisieren einlädt. Die vier hintereinander liegenden Wohnräume mit Atelier sind direkt verbunden, aber auch durch den Flur erschließbar. Die Eingangstüren stammen aus der Jugendstilepoche.

The color scheme and the confluence of art and architecture both play important roles in this mansion house, the home of the architect Anna Maske and the artist Fausto Faini. Anna Maske has created a "miniature architecture" for her daughter: a tiny world with two shops and the facades of streets and courtyards, made from her own designs and hand-painted by Gio Ponti: it is a space that encourages experimentation and improvisation. The other four inner rooms and the workshop are interconnected but they also have their own independent exit onto the corridor. The doors in the entrance are from the Jugendstil (Art Nouveau) era.

Ce logement seigneurial est occupé par l'architecte Anna Maske et l'artiste Fausto Faini. Ici, la composition chromatique entre l'art et l'architecture tient un rôle important. Anna Maske a créé pour sa fille une « architecture en miniature » : un micro cosmos peint à la main par Gio Ponti qui représente deux magasins, des rues et des cours. Cet espace invite à improviser et à expérimenter. Les quatre chambres et l'atelier communiquent entre eux et donnent sur le couloir. Les portes d'entrée sont de l'époque du Jugendstil (« modernisme »).

En esta vivienda señorial donde viven la arquitecta Anna Maske y el artista Fausto Faini, la composición cromática y la convivencia entre arte y arquitectura desempeñan un papel destacado. Anna Maske creó para su hija una arquitectura en miniatura: un diminuto cosmos con dos tiendas y fachadas de calles y patios realizado según su propio diseño y pintado a mano por Gio Ponti, espacio que invita a experimentar e improvisar. Las cuatro habitaciones interiores restantes y el taller están comunicados entre sí pero también tienen salida independiente al pasillo. Las puertas de la entrada son de la época del Jugendstil (modernismo).

Location: **Charlottenburg**
Architect: **Anna Maske**
Photos: © **concrete**

Workshop-home

Anna Maske

Kräftige Formen und Farben dominieren in dieser Altbauwohnung der Berliner Künstlerin Elvira Bach mit vier Zimmern und einer urgemütlichen Küche. Wenig Design, dafür viel Buntes und Fröhliches vom Trödel war das Motto bei der Einrichtung. Der lange großzügige Korridor wurde mit eigenen Kunstwerken sowie Werken befreundeter Künstler dekoriert. Im Wohnzimmer schaffen die bunten Einrichtungsgegenstände und ausdrucksstarken, überwiegend eigenen Objekte und Bilder eine fröhliche und positive Atmosphäre. In der behaglichen Wohnküche speist man inmitten von viel Rot, Karo und Tupfen und kann sich an den von Elvira Bach erschaffenen „Erdbeer" Siebdrucken erfreuen.

Strong forms and colors dominate the four rooms and cozy kitchen in the old apartment occupied by the Berlin artist Elvira Bach. Little formal design but abundant splashes of joyful color define the basic decorative theme. The long, broad corridor is lined with works by Bach and her artist friends. The colorful adornments in the lounge combine with the highly expressive paintings – mostly the artist's own work – to create a vivacious, optimistic atmosphere. Guests eating in the comfortable kitchen find themselves surrounded by checkers and polka dots and a wealth of red motifs, including the "strawberries" in Elvira Bach's own screenprints.

Les formes et les couleurs éclatantes prédominent dans ce vieil appartement composé de quatre chambres et d'une cuisine accueillante, et qui appartient à l'artiste berlinoise Elvira Bach. Peu de design mais en revanche plein de babioles colorées a été la ligne directrice de la décoration. Le couloir, long et large, est décoré par des œuvres d'Elvira Bach elle-même et de ses amis artistes. Dans le salon, les éléments décoratifs sont de couleur vive, comme les objets et les tableaux d'une grande expressivité, qui sont souvent de l'artiste elle-même. Tous créent une atmosphère gaie et optimiste. Dans la confortable cuisine, on mange entouré de motifs rouges, de tableaux et les poids, et l'on peut s'amuser avec les « fraises » en série graphies d'Elvira Bach.

Formas y colores llenos de fuerza dominan en el piso antiguo de cuatro habitaciones y una acogedora cocina de la artista berlinesa Elvira Bach. La consigna seguida en la decoración fue poco diseño pero, en cambio, muchos cachivaches de alegre colorido. El pasillo, largo y generoso, está decorado con obras propias y de artistas amigos. En el salón, los elementos decorativos de vivos colores así como los objetos y cuadros de gran expresividad, en su mayoría creados por la artista, logran una atmósfera alegre y optimista. En la confortable cocina uno come rodeado de muchos motivos de color rojo, cuadros y lunares, y puede regocijarse con las "fresas" serigrafiadas de Elvira Bach.

Location: **Charlottenburg**
Design: **By the residents**
Photos: **© Reto Guntli**

The joy of colour

By the residents

Die Eigentümerin dieser Wohnung hatte sich bereits gegen Ende der Planungsphase in das Bauprojekt eingekauft und konnte so an der Gestaltung ihrer Wohnung entscheidend mitwirken. Ihren individuellen Bedürfnissen entsprechend hat die Glasdesignerin ein kleines Atelier in die Wohnung integriert, ihre Werkstatt jedoch in den Keller gelegt. Durch einen großen rollbaren Schrank lässt sich das Atelier vom Wohnbereich abtrennen. Die Werkstatt erreicht man über einen direkt mit der Wohnung verbundenen Aufzug. Zwischen Wohn- und Badezimmer wurde durch ein kleines Fenster ein Sichtbezug hergestellt.

The owner of this apartment bought it at the end of the planning stage and so had the opportunity to participate decisively in its conception. Bearing in mind her individual needs, this designer of glass objects decided to fit a small studio into the apartment and put her workshop in the basement. The studio is separated from the rest of the domestic space by a huge closet on castors. The workshop is reached via an elevator that opens directly onto the apartment. The living room and bathroom are visually connected by a small window.

La propriétaire de cet appartement l'était déjà au moment de la conception des plans, et a donc pu participer activement à la réforme. Prenant en compte ses besoins personnels, cette designer d'objets en verre a décidé d'intégrer un petit atelier dans l'appartement et d'aménager au contraire le taller au sous-sol. L'atelier est séparé du reste de l'espace domestique grâce à une énorme armoire montée sur roues. On accède au taller grâce à un ascenseur qui donne directement sur l'appartement. Le salon et la salle de bain communiquent visuellement par des petites fenêtres.

La propietaria de este piso lo era ya al final de la fase de planificación, lo que le dio la oportunidad de participar decisivamente en la concepción de la vivienda. Teniendo en cuenta sus necesidades individuales, esta diseñadora de objetos de cristal decidió integrar un pequeño estudio en el piso y situar el taller en el sótano. El estudio queda separado del resto del espacio doméstico por medio de un enorme armario con ruedas. Al taller se accede por medio de un ascensor que se abre directamente al piso. La sala y el baño quedan comunicados visualmente a través de un pequeña ventana.

Location: **Mitte**
Architect: **Abcarius & Burns**
Photos: **© Ludger Paffrath**

House-workshop

101

Abcarius & Burns

Unter dem Konzept "Urban Living" verstehen die Architekten Abcarius & Burns weltoffenes und zugleich ortsgebundenes Wohnen in der Stadt in großzügigen und zeitgemäßen Wohnräumen. Traditionelle Wohnformen mit einer räumlichen Trennung der einzelnen Wohnfunktionen wie Wohn, Ess- und Badezimmer werden berücksichtigt, aber auch hinterfragt und verändert. Die verschiedenen Raumelemente werden bei der Gestaltung auf das Notwendige reduziert und klare Linien angestrebt. Eine besondere Atmosphäre soll vor allem durch das Zusammenspiel der verwendeten Materialen mit dem Licht und den Raumproportionen entstehen.

Following the concept of "Urban Living", the architects Abcarius & Burns have arrived at a form of living in a city that is cosmopolitan and local at the same time and offers generously proportioned spaces adapted to modern needs. The traditional format of separating the different domestic functions into lounge, dining room and bathroom is respected, but it is questioned and modified. The various spatial elements are reduced to bare necessities and bold, simple lines. The result is a special atmosphere, set off by the interplay between the materials used, the spatial proportions and the light.

Les architectes Abcarius & Burns entendent par le concept de « urban living », une façon à la fois cosmopolite et locale de vivre en la ville, dans de grands espaces adaptés aux temps modernes. Les modes de vie traditionnels avec la séparation des différentes fonctions domestiques en salon, salle à manger et salle de bain, sont respectés en même temps que remis en cause et modifiés. Les différents éléments spatiaux se réduisent maintenant au strict minimum et restent limités à des lignes claires et simples. Ceci crée une atmosphère spéciale, notamment grâce au jeu des matériaux utilisés, de la lumière et des dimensions spatiales.

Bajo el concepto de vida urbana, los arquitectos Abcarius & Burns entienden una forma –cosmopolita y local a un tiempo– de vivir la ciudad en espacios generosos y adaptados a los tiempos modernos. Las formas de vivir tradicionales con su separación de las diferentes funciones domésticas en salón, comedor y baño se respetan, eso sí, puestas en tela de juicio y modificadas. Los diferentes elementos espaciales se reducen ahora a lo estrictamente necesario y quedan limitados a líneas claras y sencillas. Debe lograrse crear un ambiente especial sobre todo por medio del juego entre los materiales utilizados con la luz y las proporciones espaciales.

Location: **Mitte**
Architect: **Abcarius & Burns**
Photos: © **Ludger Paffrath**

Urban Living

109

Abcarius & Burns

In dieser Wohnung steht die Funktionalität der Räume und ihrer Einrichtung im Vordergrund. Die bis zum Boden reichenden Fenster schaffen eine visuelle Einbeziehung des öffentlichen Raumes in die private Wohnung und umgekehrt. Der Küchen- und Wohnbereich bilden eine Einheit, während das Badezimmer durch eine Schiebetür räumlich und optisch abgetrennt werden kann. Die individuelle Kopplung und Trennung der Wohnfunktionen ist für die Architekten Abcarius & Burns ein wichtiges gestalterisches Mittel. Um eine optimale atmosphärische Raumqualität zu erzielen, wurden die Heizkörper und andere technische Elemente für den Bewohner unsichtbar installiert.

The main priority in this home was the functionality of the rooms and their decoration. Windows reaching to the floor succeed in creating an interaction between the outer, public space and the domestic, private one. The kitchen and sitting room form a single unit, while the bathroom can be divided off both physically and visually by means of a sliding door. The possibility of uniting and separating the domestic spaces according to personal needs is a basic creative resource for the architects Abcarius & Burns. In order to make the setting as attractive as possible, the radiators and other technical elements have been hidden from view.

On a donné priorité dans cette maison à la fonctionnalité des pièces et à celle de la décoration. Les portes-fenêtres permettent à l'espace public extérieur de communiquer avec la zone domestique privée, et vice-versa. La cuisine et le salon forment une seule unité tandis que la salle de bain peut être séparée physiquement et visuellement au moyen d'une porte coulissante. La possibilité d'unir et de séparer les espaces domestiques à sa guise a été un point fondamental pour les architectes Abcarius & Burns. Afin de parvenir à une qualité optimale de l'espace ambiant, les radiateurs et les autres éléments techniques ont été installés de façon à ne pas être vus.

En esta vivienda se dio prioridad, sobre todo, a la funcionalidad de las habitaciones y la decoración. Las ventanas hasta el suelo logran que el espacio público exterior se implique con la zona doméstica privada y viceversa. La cocina y la sala forman una unidad mientras que el baño se puede separar física y visualmente por medio de una puerta corredera. La posibilidad de unir y separar los espacios domésticos según las necesidades individuales es un recurso creativo fundamental para los arquitectos Abcarius & Burns. Con el fin de lograr una calidad espacial ambiental óptima, los radiadores de la calefacción y otros elementos técnicos se instalaron ocultos a la vista.

Location: **Mitte**
Architect: **Abcarius & Burns**
Photos: © **Ludger Paffrath**

A loft in Mitte

Abcarius & Burns

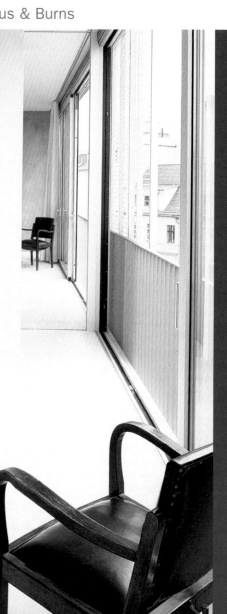

Der Privatbereich mit Schlaf- und Badezimmer wurde in dieser 2-Etagen-Dachwohnung in die untere Etage gelegt, um den schönen Dachbereich als großen und offenen Wohn- und Küchenbereich zu nutzen. Die Raumhöhe variiert von 2,75 Meter bis zu 4,80 Metern. Als Dachträger wurden gebogene Holzschichtbinder verwendet, die sichtbar vom Boden bis an die Decke streben. Die Sofaecke vor dem Kamin wurde um einige Zentimeter tiefer in den Boden gelegt, so dass der Luftraum optimal ausgenutzt wird. Im Schlafzimmer wurde das Badezimmer ohne Trennwände in den Raum integriert.

The private quarters, with the bathroom and bedroom, are on the lower floor in this two-story home, making it possible to exploit the charming space under the roof to create a large, open kitchen and living area. The ceiling varies in height from 9 feet to 16 feet at its highest point. Four wooden ribs serve as beams, running from the floor to the ceiling, completely exposed to view. The floor in the corner area with the sofa and the fireplace has been sunk a few inches lower than the rest of the floor to take full advantage of the space. The bathroom is integrated into the bedroom, without any dividing wall between the two.

La sphère privée comprenant les chambres et la salle de bain se situe à l'étage inférieur de cette maison repartie sur deux étages. On peut ainsi de profiter du bel espace que nous offre le toit pour en faire une grande zone ouverte servant de cuisine et de séjour. La hauteur du toit atteint les 4,80 m dans ses parties les plus hautes. On a choisi pour les poutres maîtresses différents cintres de bois qui s'offrent à la vue sur toute leur longueur. Le coin face à la cheminée, où se trouve le canapé, a été repris de quelques centimètres par rapport au sol pour profiter au maximum de l'espace. La salle de bain a été intégrée à la chambre sans aucun mur de séparation.

El baño y los dormitorios, o sea, la esfera privada, se situaron en el piso inferior de esta vivienda repartida entre dos plantas, de forma que se pudo aprovechar el bonito espacio del tejado para hacer una amplia y abierta zona de cocina y sala. La altura del techo va de 2,75 m hasta 4,80 m en su parte más alta. Como vigas se eligieron varias cerchas de madera que se alzan totalmente a la vista desde el suelo hasta el techo. La esquina frente a la chimenea, donde se asienta el sofá, se hundió algunos centímetros con respecto al suelo para aprovechar el espacio al máximo. El baño está integrado en el dormitorio sin ninguna pared de separación.

Location: **Mitte**
Architects: **Hoyer & Schindele**
Photos: **© concrete**

Attic in Auguststraße

Hoyer & Schindele

Dieser Neubau entstand 1999/2000 in einem Viertel von Gründerzeitbauten, die um das Jahr 1900 errichtet wurden. Das Konzept der großflächig verglasten Holzfassade beruht auf dem Verzicht von Geschlossenheit. Alle Wohnungen sind mindestens zweigeschossig und erstrecken sich sowohl zur vorderen als auch zur hinteren Fassadenseite. Eine sich aufwärts windende ovale Treppe führt zu den verschiedenen Wohneinheiten. Das von den Architekten verfolgte Ziel, rigide Wohnformen und Lebensideen aufzubrechen, ist auch bei der Gestaltung der Innenbereiche erkennbar und so gehen z. B. Schlaf- und Badezimmerbereich fließend ineinander über.

This new building was put up in 1999/2000 in the middle of a neighbourhood of mansion houses dating from 1900. The wooden facade with large windows is evidence of a brief that renounced any enclosed forms or spaces. All the homes inside occupy at least two floors and stretch to the back of the building. An oval staircase winds its way up to the various apartments. The architects' desire to break free of rigid forms and lifestyles is apparent in their conception of the interior space: the bathroom and bedroom, for example, are interconnected, with no dividing wall between them.

Cet édifice de construction récente a été bâti en 1999/2000 dans le centre d'un quartier aux demeures seigneuriales de 1900. La façade en bois répond avec ses grandes baies vitrées au refus de tout espace ou forme fermés. Tous les logements sont repartis au moins sur deux étages et donnent sur les faces opposées de l'édifice. Un escalier ovale relie en serpentant les diverses parties de la maison. La volonté des architectes de rompre avec les formes et les modes de vie rigides se traduit dans la conception de l'espace intérieur. Par exemple, la chambre et la salle de bain communiquent.

Este edificio de nueva construcción se levantó en 1999/2000 en medio de un barrio de fincas señoriales de 1900. La fachada de madera con grandes cristaleras responde al concepto de renuncia a cualquier forma o espacio cerrado. Todas las viviendas están repartidas al menos entre dos pisos y dan a las dos caras enfrentadas de la fachada. Una escalera oval asciende serpenteante hacia las diversas unidades de vivienda. El intento de los arquitectos de romper con formas e ideas de vivir rígidas se hace asimismo patente en la concepción del espacio interior. Así, por ejemplo, el dormitorio y el cuarto de baño están intercomunicados.

Die auf zwei Etagen verteilte Wohnung befindet sich in einem Ende des 18. Jahrhunderts entstandenen Gebäudeensemble, das im Laufe der Zeit für verschiedenste gewerbliche Zwecke genutzt wurde. Der Eigentümer strebte beim Um- und Ausbau der Räumlichkeiten vor allem den sensiblen Umgang mit der vorhandenen Bausubstanz und einen durchgängigen architektonischen Stil der Innenräume an. Zudem sollte der Gebäudekomplex sowohl als Wohnraum als auch zu gewerblichen Zwecken genutzt werden. Heute beherbergt das Objekt verschiedene Gastronomiebetriebe, Büroräume, Kunstgalerien, Künstlerateliers und zwei Wohnungen.

This home, spread over two floors, is part of a complex of eighteenth-century buildings which has been used for various industrial purposes over the years. The owner sought to respect the original character of the building and achieve an architectural style with open but coherent interior spaces, intended for both homes and commercial premises. In effect, this group of buildings now houses several restaurants, offices, art galleries and artists' workshops, as well as two private residences.

Cette demeure, répartie sur deux étages, est intégrée dans un complexe d'immeubles du siècle XVIII qui au cours des années a été utilisé à diverses fins industrielles. Le propriétaire tenta de respecter le caractère originel de l'immeuble et de réussir un style architectural de l'espace intérieur ouvert et cohérent. Cet espace a été pensé pour accueillir à la fois des logements et des espaces commerciaux. En effet, aujourd'hui cohabitent dans ce groupe d'immeubles des restaurants, des bureaux, des galeries d'art, ou encore des ateliers d'artistes, à côté de deux résidences particulières.

Esta vivienda, repartida entre dos plantas, se encuentra integrada en un complejo de edificios del siglo XVIII que a lo largo de los años ha sido utilizado para diversos fines industriales. El dueño intentó respetar la sustancia original del edificio y lograr un estilo arquitectónico del espacio interior abierto y coherente. Este espacio debía estar pensado para acoger a un tiempo viviendas y locales comerciales. En efecto, en la actualidad conviven en este conjunto de edificios varios locales gastronómicos, oficinas, galerías de arte y talleres de artistas junto a dos residencias particulares.

Im Bezirk Mitte zwischen Potsdamer Platz und Alexander Platz stehen vier Hochhäuser, die noch zu DDR-Zeiten errichtet wurden. Durch die zentrale Lage und atemberaubenden Ausblicken sind die Wohnungen in diesen Gebäuden heute wieder attraktiv geworden und Architekt Jens Jakob hat sich zu eigenen Zwecken eine nur 50 m² große Wohnung im 25. Stock umgebaut. Der Blick aus dieser Höhe erstreckt sich auf weite Teile Berlins. Durch die Kombination von dunklem Teakholz mit modernen hellen Einrichtungsgegenständen hat die Wohnung einen besonderen Charakter. Im Badezimmer wurden Feinsteinkacheln mit Holzmaterialien kombiniert.

Four skyscrapers put up in the era of the RDA loom over Potsdamer Platz and Alexander Platz. Their central location and spectacular views have given the homes inside these buildings a renewed attraction, leading the architect Jens Jakob to convert this tiny apartment on the 25th floor – measuring only 540 square feet – for his own use. The view from this height spans most of Berlin. The combination of dark teak with pale modern decorative elements bestows a very distinctive character on the home. The bathroom uses tiles in conjunction with various types of wood.

Dans le quartier de Mitte, entre la place de Potsdam et celle d'Alexander, s'élèvent quatre gratte-ciels bâtis à l'époque de la RDA. Grâce à leur emplacement central et à leur vue impressionnante, les appartements de ces immeubles sont aujourd'hui très à la mode. C'est pourquoi l'architecte Jens Jakob a réhabilité pour son usage personnel un petit appartement de seulement 50m² au 25ème étage. La vue depuis cet étage embrase une grande partie de Berlin. La combinaison du bois foncé de tec et des éléments décoratifs modernes aux tons clairs, donne à l'appartement un caractère très spécial. Dans la salle de bain, on a utilisé des petits carreaux de céramique et différents types de bois.

En el barrio de Mitte, entre la plaza de Potsdam y la plaza de Alexander, se alzan cuatro rascacielos levantados en tiempos de la RDA. Gracias a su céntrica situación y sus impresionantes vistas, las viviendas de estos edificios vuelven a resultar hoy muy atractivas. Por ello, el arquitecto Jens Jakob ha reformado para uso propio este pequeño apartamento de sólo 50 m² en el piso 25. La vista desde estas alturas se extiende sobre gran parte de Berlín. La combinación de la oscura madera de teca con elementos decorativos modernos de tonos claros da a la vivienda un carácter muy especial. En el baño se usaron losetas de cerámica junto a diferentes tipos de madera.

Location: **Mitte**
Architect: **Jens Jakob**
Photos: **© Ludger Paffrath**

Mini-apartment in Mitte

Jens Jakob

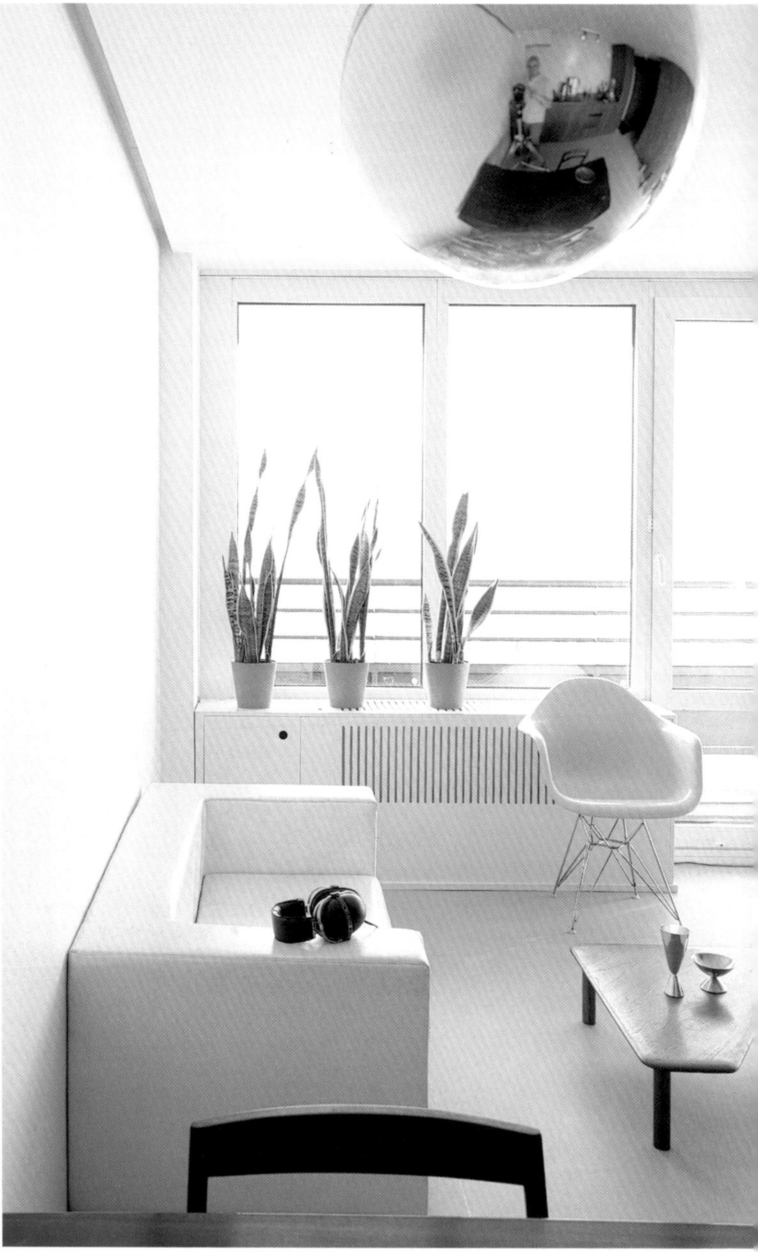

Dieses Miniapartment ist ein hervorragendes Beispiel für die gelungene Umgestaltung einer ehemaligen DDR-Plattenbauwohnung. In den ewig langen eintönigen Korridoren reiht sich ein Apartment ans Andere und so nannte man diese Wohnungen zu DDR-Zeiten auch „Arbeiterschließfächer". Der Blick aus dem 12. Stock ist atemberaubend und schafft zudem zusätzlich „Raum", den man sich jedoch mit dem Auge erobern muss. Das Bett lässt sich rollen und so je nach Bedarf auch einfach mal unters Fenster stellen, um ganz gemütlich den herrlichen Blick auf das geschichtsträchtige rote Rathaus zu genießen. Die Einrichtung ist v. a. im Stil der 60er gehalten und wurde auf wenige ausgewählte Objekte reduziert.

This tiny apartment is a good example of the successful conversion of a home in one of the prefabricated gray blocks that were typical in East Germany. The apartments, popularly known as "lockers", were ranged along endless, monotonous corridors. The view from the twelfth floor is stunning and acts almost as an extension, compensating for the lack of space inside. The bed on castors can be placed next to the window to relax and enjoy the beautiful view of the historic red City Hall building. The decoration is inspired by the 1960s and is restricted to a few carefully chosen elements.

Ce minuscule appartement, situé dans un des blocs en ciment gris préfabriqués caractéristiques de l'ancienne RDA, est l'exemple d'une rénovation réussie. Dans d'interminables couloirs monotones s'alignaient les appartements, connus aussi sous le nom de « casiers ». La vue du 12ème étage est saisissante et offre une étendue extraordinaire à notre regard. Le lit sur roues peut être placé près de la fenêtre pour profiter tout à notre aise de la merveilleuse vue sur l'historique bâtiment rouge de la mairie. La décoration est inspirée du style des années 60 et se limite à peu d'objets, tous savamment sélectionnés.

Este minúsculo apartamento es un buen ejemplo de la lograda remodelación de un piso de los característicos bloques grises prefabricados de la antigua RDA. A lo largo de interminables y monótonos pasillos se alineaban los apartamentos, conocidos popularmente como "taquillas". La vista desde el piso 12 es sobrecogedora y proporciona un espacio extraordinario que hay que conquistar con la mirada. La cama con ruedas se puede colocar junto a la ventana para disfrutar cómodamente de la hermosa vista sobre el histórico edificio rojo del Ayuntamiento. La decoración está inspirada en el estilo de los años sesenta y se limita a pocos objetos cuidadosamente elegidos.

Location: **Mitte**
Design: **By the resident**
Photos: **© E. Wentorf**

The beehive

159

By the resident

Dieses Loft befindet sich in einer alten Remise in Berlin Mitte aus dem Jahre 1860 und dient gleichermaßen als Wohnort und Atelier. Das Gebäude wurde in alten Zeiten als Pferdestall genutzt und das vor einigen Jahren als Wohn- und Arbeitsraum ausgebaute Dachgeschoss diente der Heulagerung. Bei der Renovierung wurde die alte Stahl- und Holzbalkenkonstruktion und der außen vorhandene Lastaufzug erhalten, für ausreichende Lichtzufuhr sorgt eine moderne Dachfensterkonstruktion. Die vorherrschende Farbe Weiß schafft eine helle und freundliche Atmosphäre, farbliche Auflockerung bringen die geometrischen und bunten Kunstwerke von Ottmar Lerche und der selbst angemalte Estrichboden.

This building, an outhouse in the heart of Berlin dating from 1860, was originally a stable with a loft; the latter was then used as a granary, before being converted into a home and workplace a few years ago. The conversion preserved the old structure, with its wood and steel beams, as well as the hoist outside. The insertion of skylights allows light to flow into the interior and the predominance of white creates a luminous and welcoming atmosphere. As a counterpoint, splashes of color are provided by both the geometrical patterns of Ottmar Lerche's paintings and the cement floor, which he has decorated himself.

Cet immeuble, un entrepôt de 1860 situé en plein centre de Berlin, était une écurie dont grenier qui servait à l'origine de grange, a été transformé il y a quelques années en logement et lieu de travail. La structure originelle, les poutres en acier et en bois ainsi que le monte-charge extérieur ont été conservés lors des travaux. La présence de lucarnes permet le passage de la lumière, et la couleur blanche qui prédomine crée une atmosphère lumineuse et accueillante. En contrepartie, les œuvres géométriques de Ottmar Lerche, d'une grande richesse chromatique, ainsi que le sol en ciment décoré par l'artiste, apportent une touche de couleur à l'appartement.

Este edificio, un cobertizo de 1860 situado en pleno centro de Berlín, era una caballeriza y su desván, reconvertido hace algunos años en vivienda y lugar de trabajo, servía originalmente de granero. En la reforma, se conservaron la vieja estructura de vigas de acero y madera y el montacargas exterior. La construcción de claraboyas permite el paso de la luz y el color blanco predominante crea una atmósfera luminosa y acogedora. Como contrapunto, las obras geométricas de gran riqueza cromática de Ottmar Lerche y el suelo de cemento ornamentado por el mismo artista ponen la nota de color.

Location: **Mitte**
Design: **By the resident**
Photos: **© E. Wentorf**

Home-workshop

By the resident

Bei diesem Dachausbau war das Ziel des Architekten in erster Linie, den fantasti-schen Ausblick auf die Stadt zu nutzen sowie die ursprünglich nach Norden und zur Straße hin gelegenen Wohnbereiche so umzuorientieren, dass sie jetzt zum sonni-gen Süden und Gartenbereich liegen. Die Dachterrasse mit ihrer extravaganten Form lädt zu einer Pause mit Blick auf den berühmten Alexanderplatz ein. Im Innen-bereich wird durch eine gezielte Farbgestaltung der verschiedenen Raumelemente und die funktionale und reduzierte Einrichtung eine besondere Raumerfahrung her-vorgerufen. Eine geschwungene, zentral angeordnete begehbare Raumplastik ver-bindet die erste und zweite Etage des Wohnbereiches.

Here the architect's main aim was to enhance the fantastic views of the city from this roof-top home, which originally looked northwards onto the street but now, after its conversion, faces south to take advantage of the sunlight and the garden. The flam-boyantly designed terrace is ideal for relaxing and enjoying the view of the famous Alexandersplatz. Inside, the carefully balanced colors of the different spatial ele-ments, along with the minimal and functional decoration, create a very special at-mosphere. A curved central partition links the two floors in the home.

Le principal objectif de l'architecte a été d'offrir à ce logement construit sur une ter-rasse, une vue imprenable sur la ville. Les travaux ont consisté à réorienter au sud l'appartement qui donnait initialement sur la rue. La terrasse, de forme extravagan-te, invite au repos et donne sur la fameuse Place Alexander. Les espaces intérieurs, peints différemment mais avec harmonie, ainsi que la décoration minimaliste et fonctionnelle, créent une atmosphère très spéciale. Une esthétique spatiale cohé-rente aux formes courbes et faciles d'accès, unit les deux étages de l'appartement.

El objetivo del arquitecto fue, sobre todo, potenciar las fantásticas vistas sobre la ciudad de esta vivienda construida en la azotea y vuelta en un principio hacia el nor-te y la calle, y reorientarla en el nuevo proyecto hacia el soleado sur y el jardín. La azotea, de extravagante forma, invita a tomarse un descanso y disfrutar de la vis-ta sobre la famosa plaza Alexander. En el interior, una cuidada composición de co-lor de los diferentes elementos espaciales así como la decoración, mínima y fun-cional, crean un ambiente muy especial. Una plástica espacial centrada, de formas curvas y transitable une los dos pisos del espacio de vivienda.

Rooftop Lottumstraße

Stefan Sterf

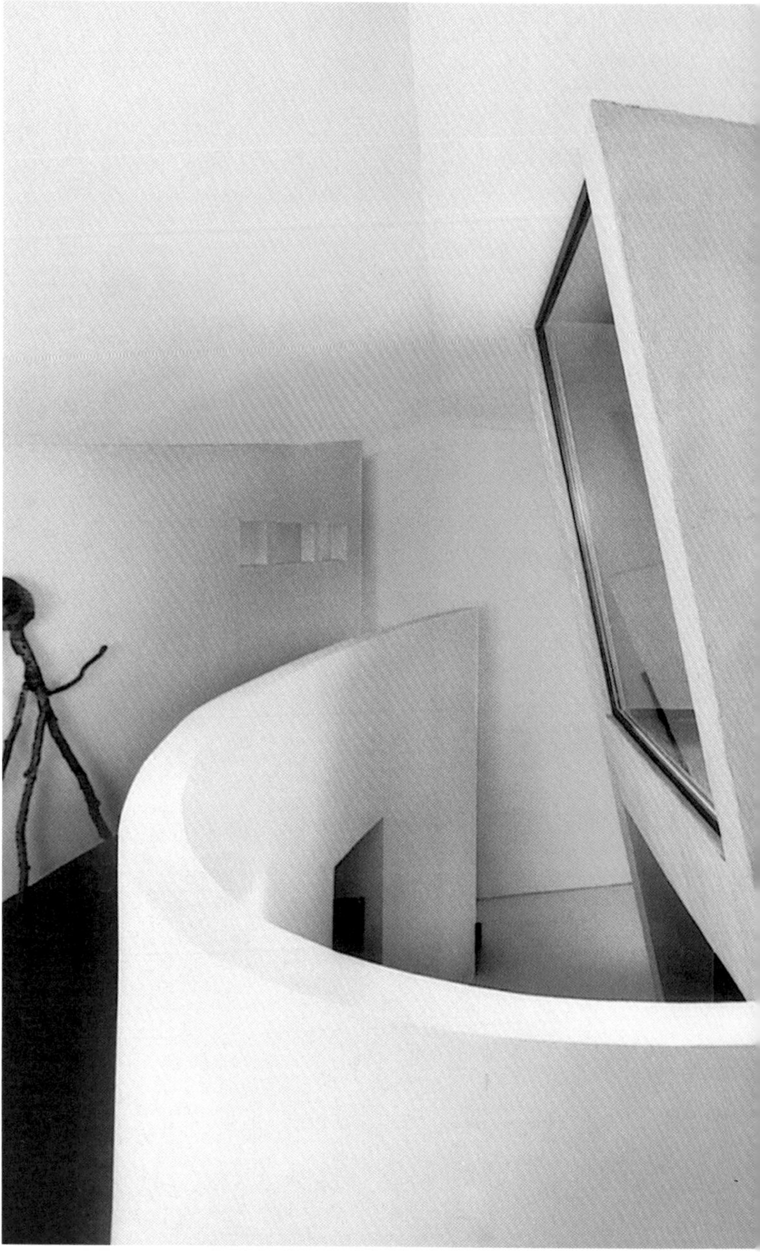

Sections

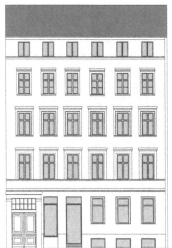

Front elevation

Rear elevation

Dieses Loft befindet sich im 3. Stock eines sanierten und industriell genutzten Gewerbebaus aus der Jahrhundertwende, dessen durchgehendes Backsteinmauerwerk sowohl bei der Fassade als auch im Innenbereich erhalten wurde. Um die Authentizität des Materials zu erhalten wurden alle Elektroleitungen, Steckdosen und Schalter in den aus gegossenen Estrichplatten bestehenden beheizbaren Boden gelegt. Küche und Bad sind ohne zusätzliche Raumteiler frei im Loft verteilt und das mittig in den Raum platzierte WC stellt besonders bei abendlicher gezielter Lichtführung geradezu ein schmückendes Kunstobjekt dar. Die Küchenelemente wie auch andere Möbelobjekte lassen sich nach Bedarf verschieben.

This loft is situated on the third floor of a late-nineteenth century industrial building whose superbly finished brickwork was left exposed, both inside and on the facade, after its refurbishment. To ensure that the materials retained their authentic look, the electrical wiring, sockets, switches and even the heating were set in the cement floor. The kitchen and bathroom are left open, without any separation from the rest of the space, and the toilet in the center becomes a decorative object, especially in the carefully planned night-time lighting. The kitchen units and some of the furniture can be moved around as required.

Ce loft se trouve au troisième étage d'un entrepôt datant de la fin du XIX siècle, dans lequel on a conservé après rénovation les murs aussi bien intérieurs qu'extérieurs. Afin de préserver l'authenticité des matériaux, les câbles électriques, les prises de courant, les interrupteurs et même le chauffage ont été enfouis dans le sol en ciment. La cuisine et la salle de bain sont librement aménagées sans être coupées du reste de l'appartement. De cette façon, le soir, les toilettes, éclairés et placés au centre de l'appartement, deviennent objet de décoration. Les éléments de la cuisine et certains meubles peuvent être réagancés comme on le souhaite.

Este loft se encuentra en el tercer piso de una nave industrial de finales del XIX, tras cuya reforma se conservaron los muros de ladrillo tanto de la fachada como del interior. Para salvar la autenticidad del material, los cables eléctricos, tomas de corriente, interruptores e incluso la calefacción se integraron en el suelo de cemento. La cocina y el baño están dispuestos libremente sin ninguna separación del resto del ambiente. Así, sobre todo bajo la cuidada iluminación nocturna, la taza del baño situada en el centro se convierte en un objeto decorativo. Los elementos de la cocina y algunos de los muebles se pueden recolocar según convenga.

Location: **Prenzlauer Berg**
Architect: **Grollmitz-Zappe**
Photos: **© Kirsti Kriegel**

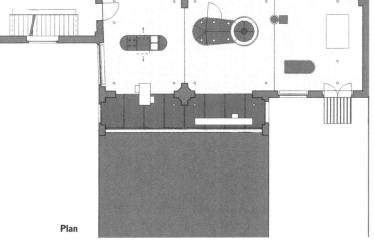

Plan

Bei der Modernisierung dieses Gründerzeitbaus in den Jahren 1998 und 1999 wurde der Dachbereich geöffnet und durch eine umlaufende Terrasse ein großer Außenbereich geschaffen. Die vielen und zum großen Teil bis an den Boden reichenden Fenster sorgen für eine helle und freundliche Atmosphäre. Im Wohnzimmer laden eine Sitzgruppe und die frei im Raum verteilten großen Kissen zu einem gemütlichen Verweilen mit Blick auf den bepflanzten Außenbereich ein. Die Einrichtung ist minimalistisch und es wurden Objekte verschiedener Stilrichtungen miteinander kombiniert. Der Holzboden ist ein Massivholzparkett aus Kirsche.

The modernization of this Gründerzeit-style building, carried out between 1998 and 1999, opened up the roof area and created a large outdoors area in the form of a make the setting luminous and welcoming. The big cushions scattered freely all over the sitting room invite visitors to relax and enjoy the view of the terrace, with its profusion of plants. The decoration is minimalist and combines objects from different styles. The floor is covered with solid cherry wood parquet.

Durant la modernisation de cette construction de style Gründerzeit, réalisée entre 1998 et 1999, on a ouvert le toit et on a créé au moyen d'une terrasse en suite, un grand espace extérieur. Les nombreuses fenêtres, dont beaucoup arrivent jusqu'au sol, créent une atmosphère claire et accueillante. Dans le salon, un espace pour s'asseoir et de grands coussins librement disposés dans toute la pièce permettent de profiter confortablement de la vue sur l'extérieur, oú se trouvent plein de plantes. La décoration est minimaliste et combine des objets de différents styles. Le sol est recouvert de parquet de bois de cerisier.

En la modernización de esta construcción de estilo Gründerzeit, llevada a cabo entre los años 1998 y 1999, se abrió la zona del tejado y por medio de una terraza corrida se creó un gran espacio exterior. Las numerosas ventanas, muchas de ellas abiertas hasta el suelo, proporcionan un ambiente claro y acogedor. En el salón, una zona habilitada para sentarse y los grandes cojines repartidos libremente por toda la habitación invitan a disfrutar cómodamente de la vista al espacio exterior cuajado de plantas. La decoración es minimalista y combina objetos de diferentes estilos. El suelo está recubierto de parquet de madera de cerezo maciza.

Dieses Loft befindet sich in einer ehemaligen Schokoladenfabrik und die 250 m² Wohnfläche erstrecken sich über zwei Etagen. Das schöne alte Ziegelmauerwerk wurde bewahrt und weiß angestrichen. Drei Aufgänge sorgen für eine bequeme Verbindung der beiden Etagen in allen Teilen der Wohnung. Die untere Etage dient als offener Küchen- und Wohnbereich mit vielen Holzmöbeln, im oberen Bereich liegen die Schlafräume und ein riesiges Badezimmer mit offener Dusche, einer übergroßen Badewanne und einer Sauna. Überall schmücken Kunstwerke die Wände und ein beidseitig bemaltes Bild auf Rollen kann je nach Bedarf platziert werden.

This 2,700-square foot loft, situated in an old chocolate factory, is spread over two floors. The beautiful old brick wall has been preserved and painted white. All the living areas on both the floors are conveniently interconnected by means of three access points. The lower story houses an open kitchen and sitting room replete with wooden furniture. The upper story contains the bedrooms and the enormous bathroom with an open shower, a large tub and a sauna. The walls are dotted with works of art, while a screen, with castors that enable it to be positioned as required, sports a painting on both sides.

Ce loft est une ancienne usine de chocolat dont les 250 m² se répartissent sur deux étages. Le vieux et beau mur en brique a été conservé et peint en blanc. Toutes les zones d'habitation des deux étages communiquent entre elles grâce à trois accès. L'étage inférieur comprend la cuisine et un salon ouvert avec de nombreux meubles en bois. A l'étage supérieur, se trouvent les chambres et l'immense salle de bain, qui comprend une douche ouverte, une baignoire et un sauna. Les murs sont tous décorés avec des œuvres d'art tandis qu'un tableau peint des deux côtés et monté sur roues peut être placé ou bon nous semble.

Este loft está en una antigua fábrica de chocolates y sus 250 m² se reparten en dos plantas. El viejo y bello muro de ladrillo se conservó y se pintó de blanco. Todas las zonas de vivienda de ambos pisos están comunicadas cómodamente entre sí por tres accesos. El piso de abajo acoge una cocina y un salón abiertos y con muchos muebles de madera. En la planta superior están los dormitorios y el enorme cuarto de baño con una ducha abierta, una bañera de grandes dimensiones y una sauna. Las paredes están decoradas por doquier con obras de arte, y un cuadro pintado por ambos lados y montado sobre ruedas puede colocarse donde se desee.

Loft in Neukölln

Michael Krech

1 20 m² Wohnfläche bietet diese 1993 ausgebaute Dachwohnung, wo sich früher einmal der für alle Hausbewohner zugängliche Trockenboden für die Wäsche befand. Das Gebäude stammt aus dem Ende des 19. Jahrhunderts. Die besondere Holzstruktur der ehemaligen Brandschutzwände verleiht dem Loft einen besonderen Charakter. Besonders im Schlafzimmer und in der Essecke wird das Raumgefühl stark durch die fachwerkartigen Wände beeinflusst. Bei abendlicher Beleuchtung ist der kleine orangegelb angeleuchtete Treppenaufgang mit Zugang zu einem kleinen Studio ein schöner Blickfang. Das moderne Küchenmobiliar aus schwarzem Granit wurde auf Maß eingebaut.

This home, built in 1993 in a garret formerly used by the occupants of the building to dry clothes, revels in a floor space of 1,300 square foot. The building itself dates from the late nineteenth century. The fireproofed walls have been preserved, endowing the loft with a very special atmosphere. The masonry of the walls both define and enhance the sense of space, especially in the bedroom and dining room. The stairs going up to the little studio attract the attention at night on account of their yellowish-orange lighting. The modern black granite kitchen furniture was specially commissioned.

Cet appartement, construit en 1933 dans une mansarde qui servait à étendre le linge, fait 120 m² de superficie. L'immeuble date de la fin du XIXème siècle. Le coffrage contre les incendies a été conservé et confère au loft une atmosphère très spéciale. Surtout dans la chambre et la salle à manger, les murs maçonnés définissent et déterminent la sensation spatiale. Le soir, l'éclairage jaune orangé des escaliers qui mènent au petit studio, capte notre regard. Le mobilier moderne en granit noir de la cuisine à été fait sur mesure.

Esta vivienda construida en 1993 en el sotabanco de la casa, que los vecinos utilizaban antaño para tender la ropa, cuenta con una superficie de 120 m². El edificio es de finales del siglo XIX. El encofrado antiincendios de la pared se ha conservado y dota al loft de una atmósfera muy especial. Sobre todo en el dormitorio y en el comedor, las paredes definen y determinan la sensación espacial. Por la noche, la escalerita de ascenso que conduce a un pequeño estudio cautiva la mirada gracias a su iluminación en tonos naranja amarillentos. El moderno mobiliario de cocina de granito negro fue encargado a medida.

Location: **Prenzlauer Berg**
Architect: **Stephan Dass**
Photos: **© Wini Sulzbach**

Attic Kollwitz Platz

207

Stephan Dass

210

Die Maisonettewohnung befindet sich in einem Gründerzeitbau aus dem Jahre 1880 im Bezirk Prenzlauer Berg, der Ende der 90er Jahre von den Architekten Hoyer & Schindele um- und ausgebaut wurde. Das Ziel war in erster Linie, im Inneren der Häuser die architektonische Umgestaltung bewusst von dem Charakter des Altbaus abzuheben und somit ein Gegenüber und Miteinander von Neu und Alt innerhalb eines Raumgefüges zu schaffen. Das überwiegend in den Farben Weiß und Beige gehaltene Küchen- und Badezimmermobiliar und die vielen hellen Einrichtungsgegenstände sorgen im harmonischen Zusammenspiel mit den verschiedenen Holzböden für eine freundliche und warme Atmosphäre.

This garret, situated in a building in the Prenzlauer Berg neighborhood dating from 1880, was refurbished in the late 90s by the architects Hoyer & Schindele. The main aim was to distance the architectural conversion of the interior from the aristocratic style of the building to create an interplay between old and new within the same space. The kitchen and bathroom furniture – white and beige for the most part – and the host of other decorative elements in pale colors complement the various wooden floors to create a warm and cozy atmosphere.

Cette mansarde se trouve dans un immeuble du quartier de Prenzlauer Berg, qui date de 1880 et qui a été réhabilité à la fin des années 1990 par les architectes Hoyer & Schindele. L'objectif premier a été de faire ressortir le remodelage architectural intérieur au caractère seigneurial de l'immeuble, pour réunir au sein du même espace, complémentarité et contraste entre l'ancien et le moderne. Le mobilier de la salle de bain et de la cuisine, essentiellement blanc et beige, ainsi que de nombreux autres éléments décoratifs dans des tons clairs, créent en harmonie avec les différents parquets, une ambiance chaleureuse et accueillante.

Esta buhardilla se encuentra en una finca del barrio de Prenzlauer Berg original del año 1880, que fue rehabilitada a finales de la década de 1990 por los arquitectos Hoyer & Schindele. El objetivo era en primer lugar desvincular la remodelación arquitectónica del interior del carácter señorial de la finca para buscar así, en un mismo espacio, la complementariedad y el contraste entre antiguo y moderno. El mobiliario de baño y cocina, blancos y beiges en su mayor parte, y otros muchos elementos decorativos en tonos también claros crean, en armonía con los diferentes suelos de maderas, un ambiente cálido y acogedor.

Ein dominierendes Element dieser Wohnung ist die ungewöhnliche Treppenkonstruktion, die eine Verbindung zwischen 1. und 2. Etage schafft. Um in der sonst offenen Maisonettewohnung zumindest ein abgeschlossenes Raumelement zu integrieren, entschied man sich für eine Wendeltreppe mit Glashaus, deren Treppenlauf entgegen der sonst üblichen architektonischen Bauweise weder rund noch gerade, sondern eher geschwungen verläuft. Die Glaswände sorgen dafür, dass der Sichtbezug zu den Räumlichkeiten erhalten bleibt. Die verlängerte Stahlleiste der Treppe ragt über den Boden der 2. Etage hinaus und dient als drehbare Konsole für den Fernseher.

One of the dominant elements of this home is the extraordinary staircase construction joining the first and second stories. In order to integrate at least one enclosed space into this otherwise completely open garret, a spiral staircase was built inside a glass box; its sinuous curves contrast with the other – conventional and rectilinear – architectural forms. The glass walls also make it possible to enjoy the view on the far side from the interior of the apartment. The metal bar that serves as the axis of the staircase continues past the second floor to act as a revolving support for the television set.

L'élément clef de cette maison est l'extraordinaire escalier qui unit le premier et le deuxième étage. Afin d'intégrer au moins un espace clos dans cette mansarde totalement ouverte, on a construit un escalier en colimaçon dans une cage de verre, dont les formes sinueuses suivent le reste de la construction architecturale, relativement conventionnelle, non pas en courbe, mais en ligne droite. Les murs en verre permettent de profiter de la vue sur la salle de séjour. La barre de métal, colonne vertébrale de l'escalier, dépasse du sol au deuxième étage et sert de support giratoire à la télévision.

Un elemento dominante en esta vivienda es la extraordinaria construcción de la escalera, que une el primer y segundo piso. Para integrar al menos un espacio cerrado en esta buhardilla completamente abierta, se construyó una escalera de caracol con caja de cristal, cuyas formas sinuosas se dirigen contra el resto de la construcción arquitectónica, por lo demás convencional, no en curva, sino en línea recta. Las paredes de cristal permiten seguir disfrutando de la vista sobre la estancia. La barra de metal, espina dorsal de la escalera, sobresale del suelo del segundo piso y sirve de soporte giratorio sobre el que descansa la televisión.

Location: **Prenzlauer Berg**
Architects: **Hoyer & Schindele**
Photos: **© concrete**

Two-story home

Hoyer & Schindele

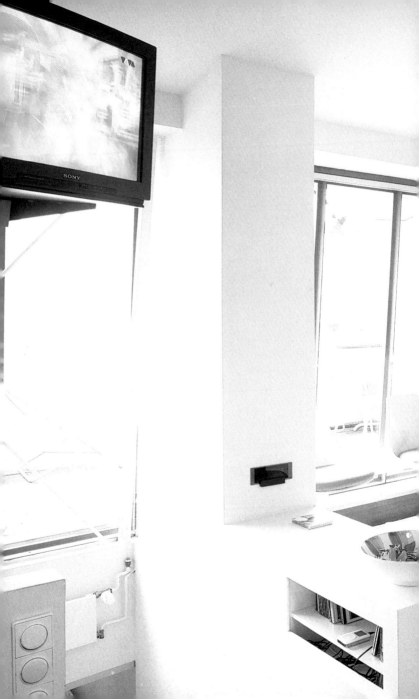

Die 140 m² Wohnfläche dieser sanierten Altbauwohnung aus der Gründerzeit resultiert aus der Zusammenlegung zweier kleinerer Wohnungen. Um den in vielen Altbauten üblichen dunklen und kleinen Badezimmertrakt attraktiver zu gestalten, wurde der Raum zum Schlafzimmer hin geöffnet. Die ursprüngliche Zugangstür im Wohnungsflur hat man geschlossen und somit das Badezimmer in den Privatbereich integriert. Die gestreifte Samttapete im Schlafzimmer ist ein Original aus den 60er Jahren. Im Wohnzimmer werden durch zwei verschiedene Vorhänge aus leichten Materialien auf nebeneinander liegenden Schienen, je nach Wunsch, unterschiedliche Lichteffekte und Raumeindrücke erzielt.

The 1,500 square feet of this original apartment in the German architectural style typical of the period 1870–1900 are the result of joining together two homes. To make the bathroom – small and dark, as is usually the case in such buildings – more attractive, the original door onto the corridor was closed. It now opens onto the bedroom as an integral part of this private space. The striped velvety wallpaper dates back to the 1960s. In the sitting room two different curtains, made of light materials, can be drawn as required by means of two parallel runners, creating a variety of lighting and spatial effects.

Cet appartement fait partie de la période architecturale allemande comprise entre 1870–1900. Les 140 m² nous viennent du regroupement de deux logements. La salle de bain, petite et obscure comme souvent dans ce genre de logements, a été rénovée. La porte qui donnait sur le couloir a été condamnée et l'accès se fait maintenant par la chambre à coucher. Le papier peint en velours est identique à ceux des années 60. Dans le salon, les deux rideaux faits de matériaux légers peuvent être tirés sur des tringles parallèles. On obtient de cette façon des effets lumineux et des sensations spatiales différentes.

Los 140 m² de este piso original del periodo arquitectónico alemán de los años 1870–1900 son el resultado de unir dos viviendas. Para hacer más atractivo el cuarto de baño, pequeño y oscuro como suele ser habitual en estas fincas, se cerró la puerta original que daba al pasillo. El baño, abierto ahora al dormitorio, quedó integrado en el entorno privado. El papel de la pared a rayas aterciopeladas es original de los años 60. En el salón, dos cortinas diferentes hechas de materiales ligeros se pueden extender según se desee por medio de dos correderas paralelas para lograr así efectos luminosos y sensaciones espaciales diferentes.

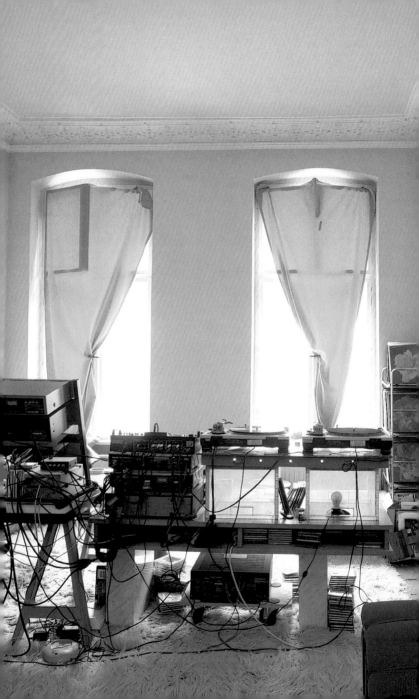

Viele Ur- und Wahlberliner hat es nach dem Mauerfall in den ehemaligen Ostbezirk Prenzlauer Berg gezogen, der sich in den letzten Jahren immer mehr zum Tummelplatz der jungen Modernen und Kreativen entwickelt hat. Es gibt viele interessante Projekte wie diese Ladenwohnung der Raumausstatterin Katja Dierssen. Als „Neuberlinerin" hatte sie die Idee, ihre 106 m² große Parterrewohnung auch als Ladenlokal zu verwenden und so unterliegt ihre Wohnung, mit Ausnahme des Schlafzimmers, auch einem ständigen Wandel. Fast alle Einrichtungsgegenstände sind käuflich, wobei die Objekte meist aus den 60er und 70er Jahre stammen.

Since the demolition of the Wall, both born-and-bred Berliners and newcomers have been attracted to the Prenzlauer Berg neighbourhood, formerly in the East and now a meeting point for creative, modern young people and a focal point for interesting design projects, such as this one by Katja Dierssen. This adopted Berliner had the idea of using her 1,140 square foot ground-floor residence as a commercial outlet. So, all the house, apart from the bedroom, is in a constant state of flux and almost all the decorative elements – mostly from the 1960s and 1970s – are for sale.

Les berlinois, aussi bien ceux de naissance que ceux d'adoption, se sentent attirés depuis la chute du mur par le quartier de Prenzlauer Berg. Autrefois du côté est, ce quartier est maintenant le lieu de rencontre de jeunes modernes et créatifs. D'intéressants projets comme celui de la décoratrice d'intérieur Katja Dierssen s'y développent. Cette berlinoise d'adoption a eu l'idée de faire d'un logement de 106 m² situé au rez-de-chaussée, un local commercial. Ainsi, à l'exception de la chambre à coucher, le reste de la maison est soumis à de constantes transformations et pratiquement tous les éléments de décoration (la plupart des années 60 et 70) sont en vente.

Berlineses de toda la vida y de adopción se han sentido atraídos tras la caída del Muro por el barrio de Prenzlauer Berg, antaño en el lado oriental y actualmente centro de reunión de jóvenes modernos y creativos, en el que se desarrollan interesantes proyectos como el de la decoradora de interiores Katja Dierssen. Esta "nueva berlinesa" tuvo la idea de utilizar la vivienda de 106 m² situada en una planta baja como local comercial. Así, con excepción del dormitorio, el resto de la casa se encuentra sometido a constantes transformaciones y casi todos los elementos decorativos, en su mayoría de los años 60 y 70, están a la venta.

Location: **Prenzlauer Berg**
Design: **By the resident**
Photos: © **E. Wentorf**

Store and home

241

By the resident

Diese 110 m^2 große Wohnung bildet ein Sammelsurium von Kuriositäten und schon beim Betreten des noch nicht sanierten und von Kriegsschäden gezeichneten Gebäudes kann man sich in das „Berlin vor dem Mauerfall" zurückversetzt fühlen. Hier herrscht kein Luxus und der bröckelnde Putz, der blanke Estrichboden sowie die alte Ofenheizung, die in den bitterkalten Monaten als Wärmezufuhr dient, und auch das improvisierte Badezimmer, bezeugen es. Doch die Wohnung hat Charme, denn der Großteil der Einrichtung wurde mit viel Liebe zum Detail auf Trödelmärkten zusammengesucht oder sogar auf speziellen Wunsch hin angefertigt und lädt zum Träumen ein.

This 1,200 square foot apartment houses a collection of knickknacks and as soon as one enters the building – which has not been refurbished and still bears the scars of war – one seems to be taken back to the Berlin that existed prior to the dismantling of the Wall. Luxury has no place here, as testified by the broken plaster on the wall, the bare floor, the old stove (still used in winter) and the improvised bathroom. Nevertheless, the house has great charm, as most of the decorative objects were lovingly chosen in flea markets or specially commissioned, and they create a highly evocative atmosphere.

Cet appartement de 110 m^2 habrite une collection de curisosités. Lorsqu'on pénètre dans l'immeuble, qui n'a pas été restauré et qui est resté marqué par la guerre, on se sent transportés dans le Berlin antérieur à la chute du mur. Ici, le luxe ne règne pas. Le prouvent les murs décrépis, le sol sans revêtement, le vieux poêle qui sert encore pour les jours froids et la salle de bain improvisée. Néanmoins, la maison reste charmante, étant donné que la plupart des objets de décoration ont été choisis avec amour aux puces et dans les petits marchés. Certains ont été commandés spécialement pour la maison, et tous créent une atmosphère qui invite au rêve.

Este piso de 110 m^2 alberga toda una colección de curiosidades y ya en el mismo momento de entrar en el edificio, sin restaurar y aún marcado por la guerra, se siente uno transportado al Berlín anterior a la caída del Muro. Aquí no impera el lujo y las paredes desconchadas, el suelo de pavimento desnudo, la vieja estufa que aún se utiliza en los meses fríos, así como el improvisado cuarto de baño, lo corroboran. Sin embargo, la casa tiene mucho encanto, ya que la mayor parte de los objetos de decoración fueron seleccionados con mimo en rastros y mercadillos o bien encargados expresamente, y crean una atmósfera que invita a soñar.

By the resident

Dieses Loft im ehemaligen Ostberliner Bezirk Prenzlauer Berg befindet sich in einem alten Postgebäude, welches zum Zeitpunkt, als es seine Bewohner entdeckten, bereits fünf Jahre leer stand. Im Jahre 1998 mieteten die heutigen vier Bewohner die ehemalige Verwaltungsetage der Post im ersten Stock an und teilten die Fläche von 300 m^2 in fünf Zimmer auf. Für jeden Bewohner wurde ein Privatbereich von 25 m^2 geschaffen und die restliche Fläche als Loft belassen und für die gemeinsame Nutzung als Wohnbereich gestaltet. Die alten an den Decken verlaufenden Kabelkanäle und Heizungsrohre wurden aus optischen Gründen zum größten Teil erhalten und sind noch in Gebrauch.

This loft in the old Prenzlauer Berg neighbourhood in East Berlin is situated in a former post office building that was unoccupied for five years before its conversion. In 1998 the four current tenants rented the first floor, once the post office's administrative department, and they divided the 3,230 square foot floor space into five areas. Each created a private 270 square foot room, while the rest was left for communal use. Most of the old cabling and the heating pipes on the ceiling – still used today – were left exposed for esthetic reasons.

Ce loft du quartier Est Prenzlauer Berg de Berlin, installé dans un ancien bâtiment de la poste, est resté inoccupé durant cinq années jusqu'au moment des travaux. En 1998, les quatre habitants ont loué le premier étage qui servait de bureau administratif à la poste et ont divisé les 300 m^2 en cinq espaces distincts. Dans chacun d'eux ils ont aménagé une surface privée de 25 m^2 et ont réservé le reste du loft à un espace commun. Pour des raisons esthétiques, la plupart des câbles et des tuyauteries qui courent sur le plafond ont été conservés et sont toujours utilisés aujourd'hui.

Este loft del otrora barrio de Berlín Este Prenzlauer Berg se encuentra en el interior de un antiguo edificio de Correos que llevaba cinco años desocupado hasta la reforma. En 1998, los actuales cuatro inquilinos alquilaron la primera planta, que había albergado las oficinas de la administración de Correos, y dividieron la superficie de 300 m^2 en cinco espacios. Para cada uno de ellos se creó un habitáculo privado de 25 m^2 y el resto se dejó como loft de uso común. Por razones estéticas se conservó la mayoría de los conductos del cableado y las viejas tuberías de la calefacción que recorrían el techo y que todavía hoy se utilizan.

Location: **Prenzlauer Berg**
Design: **By the residents**
Photos: © **concrete**

Old post office

255

By the residents

Durst

Biere :

Seedower

Feltener

Korn :

Applkorn

Vodka

Kümmel

Lindauer

Anis

Die ungewöhnliche Atmosphäre dieser Wohnung entsteht durch die Kombination dreier Wohn- und Raumkonzepte. Die für Berliner Gründerzeitwohnungen typischen hohen Decken, weißen Wände und hellen Dielenböden wurden mit einer Kollektion ungewöhnlicher, vom Bauherrn immer wieder neu variierter, Möbel aus den 50er und 60er Jahren kombiniert und erzeugen zusammen mit den Einbauten des Architekten eine schlüssige und spannungsreiche Wohnlandschaft. Die Aufmerksamkeit wird nicht auf die Funktionalität gelenkt, sondern auf das Ineinanderfließen der Körper, Räume und Flächen und deren je nach Standpunkt und Tageslicht unterschiedliche Erscheinungsweise.

The distinctive atmosphere in this home is the result of the merging of three different spatial and domestic concepts. The high ceilings, white walls and pale floorboards, so characteristic of the last century, combine with the owner's striking and varied collection of furniture from the 50s and 60s and, along with the contributions of the architect, create a coherent domestic landscape with a powerful visual impact. Functionality is not the main priority; instead, the emphasis is on the integration of forms, spaces and surfaces, and the way their appearance changes according to the viewpoint and lighting.

Ce logement a une atmosphère peu habituelle du fait qu'il regroupe trois espaces différemment conceptualisés. Les hauts plafonds, les murs blancs ainsi que les estrades aux tons clairs sont typiques du siècle dernier et sont associés à l'exceptionnelle collection de meubles des années 50 et 60 appartenant au maître de maison. Ces meubles, combinés au travail de l'architecte, créent un paysage domestique cohérent et plein de force. L'important ne réside pas dans la fonction mais dans l'intégration des corps, des espaces et des superficies; tout comme l'apparence peut changer selon la lumière.

La poco frecuente atmósfera de esta vivienda viene dada por la unión de tres diferentes conceptos espaciales y de vivienda. Los altos techos, las paredes blancas y las tarimas de tonos claros, característicos del siglo pasado, se combinan aquí con la rara y variada colección de muebles de los años 50 y 60 pertenecientes al dueño de la casa, lo que junto con las aportaciones del arquitecto crea un paisaje doméstico coherente y lleno de fuerza. El punto de gravedad no reside en la funcionalidad sino en la integración de cuerpos, espacios y superficies y en su apariencia cambiante dependiendo del punto de vista y de la luz.

Location: **Schöneberg**
Architect: **Holger Kleine**
Architects
Photos: © **concrete**

A 1950s-style home

Holger Kleine Architects

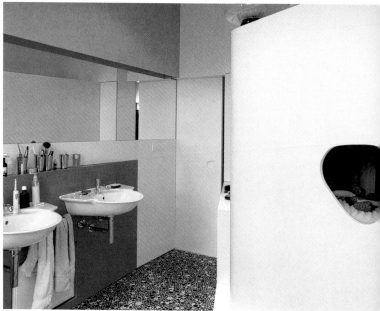

Diese 220 m² große Dachwohnung befindet sich in einem alten denkmalgeschützten Gewerbebau aus der Jahrhundertwende. Das Hinterhaus wurde von 1998–2000 saniert und in dem ehemaligen Speicherraum das Dach geöffnet und mit einer aufwendigen Lichtkuppel versehen. Gestützt wird das etwa 2,5 Tonnen schwere Atrium durch Stahlträger, die durch die ganze Wohnung verlaufen. Über eine Treppe gelangt man zur Dachterrasse. Im Badezimmer wurden Boden und Wände mit Antikmarmor gefliest. An der Außenfassade verläuft der alte Lastenfahrstuhl, der restauriert und mit einer Glaskonstruktion versehen wurde.

This 2,370 square foot attic tops an industrial building dating from the turn of the nineteenth century that is listed as a monument of national interest. The "Hinterhaus" (building with its main facade overlooking an inner courtyard) was refurbished between 1998 and 2000. The old warehouse roof was removed and replaced with a spectacular, luminous cupola. The heavy atrium, weighing 2.5 tons, was supported by steel beams spanning the whole house, while a staircase leads to the terrace. The walls and floor of the bathroom were clad with antique marble. The elevator shaft outside was restored and protected by a glass structure.

Cet attique de 220 m² se trouve dans un hangar industriel datant de la fin XIXème siècle – début du XXème siècle, et qui a été classé monument d'intérêt national. La « Hinterhaus », dont la façade principale donne sur une cour intérieure, a été réhabilitée entre 1998 et 2000. On a d'abord enlevé le toit de l'ancien entrepôt pour ensuite le recouvrir d'une spectaculaire coupole lumineuse. Le portique, qui pèse quelques 2,5 tonnes, s'appuie sur des poutres en acier qui traversent tout l'appartement. On accède à la terrasse par des escaliers. Les murs et le sol de la salle de bain ont été recouverts de vieux marbre. Sur la façade extérieure, on peut voir l'ancien monte-charge qu'on a restauré et qu'on recouvert d'une construction en verre.

Este ático de 220 m² se encuentra en una nave industrial de finales del XIX o principios del XX catalogada y protegida como monumento de interés nacional. La "Hinterhaus" –edificio con fachada principal a un patio interior– fue rehabilitada entre los años 1998 y 2000. Primero se levantó el tejado del antiguo almacén y se cubrió con una espectacular y luminosa cúpula. El pesado atrio, de unas 2,5 toneladas, se apoya en vigas de acero que cruzan toda la casa. Por medio de una escalera se sube a la azotea. Las paredes y el suelo del cuarto de baño fueron recubiertos de mármol antiguo. Por la fachada externa corre el viejo montacargas restaurado que fue recubierto de una construcción de cristal.

Location: **Kreuzberg**
Design: **By the resident**
Photos: **© Wini Sulzbach**

Attic "Hinterhaus"

271

By the resident

Für dieses Loft wurde das Treppenhaus einer ehemaligen Telefonfabrik ausgebaut und seine 123 m² Nutzfläche erstrecken sich über den 2. und 3. Stock. Zunächst gelangt man in einen in der 2. Etage gelegenen sieben Meter hohen Raum, der Teil des ehemaligen Treppenhauses ist und in dem sich jetzt die Küche befindet. Über den Küchenschrank, der auch als Treppenmöbel dient, gelangt man in eine kleine Schlafkajüte, während die Haupttreppe Zugang zu der im 3. Stock gelegenen Galerie verschafft. Eine Brücke verbindet diesen Raum mit dem Schlaf-, Arbeits- und Bibliotheksbereich und über eine weitere Treppe hat man Zugang zur Sitzlounge.

This loft was built to take advantage of the gap left by the old staircase in a telephone factory; its habitable area of 1,320 square feet is divided between the second and third floors. The entrance is by the kitchen –on the site of the building's original stairwell– which gives onto a space 23 feet high. The kitchen closet serves as steps leading up to a tiny cabin that serves as a place to sleep, while the main staircase leads to the gallery on the third floor. A bridge joins this space to the bedrooms, the office and the library, while another staircase leads to the sitting room.

Ce loft fut construit en optimisant la cage d'escalier d'une ancienne usine de téléphones. Ses 123 m² habitables se repartissent entre le deuxième et le troisième étage. On entre dans la maison par la cuisine, haute de 7 m et située au deuxième étage, qui faisait partie de l'ancienne cage d'escalier. En utilisant le placard de la cuisine comme des marches, on accède à une toute petite chambre qui sert parfois, alors que l'escalier principal conduit à la galerie du troisième étage. Un pont unit cet espace avec la zone du dortoir, du bureau et de la bibliothèque, tandis qu'un autre escalier mène au salon.

Este loft se construyó aprovechando el hueco de la escalera de una antigua fábrica de teléfonos. Sus 123 m² habitables se reparten entre el segundo y el tercer piso. A la vivienda se entra por la cocina, un espacio de 7 m de altura situado en la segunda planta, que es parte de la caja de la antigua escalera. Utilizando asimismo el armario de la cocina como peldaños, se accede a una minúscula cámara que hace las veces de dormitorio, mientras que la escalera principal conduce a la galería del tercer piso. Un puente une ese espacio con la zona del dormitorio, el despacho y la biblioteca, y una escalera más lleva a la sala de estar.

Location: **Kreuzberg**
Architect: **Peanutz Architects**
Photos: © **Thomas Bruns**

Staircase loft

279

Peanutz Architects

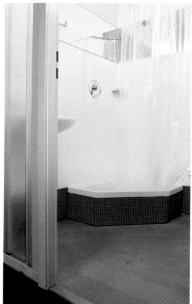

Dieses Loft auf 2 Etagen wurde als Rohbau übernommen, welcher zu einer ehemaligen Telefonfabrik gehörte. Vom Eingangsbereich mit Gästebad gelangt man über eine kleine Treppe in den sich nach oben erweiternden Badezimmerkörper, welcher den oberen Raum in Wohn- und Schlafbereich aufteilt. Der Einbau beherbergt zudem verschiedene Stauräume, Geräte und Installationen. Über die Haupttreppe hat man direkten Zugang zum Küchen- und Wohnzimmerbereich, in dem man an einem Schrankgebilde mit darrüberschwebendem Fernseher zum Küchentresen gelangt. Über diesem befindet sich ein freischwebendes „Ufo", welches sowohl als Lichtquelle als auch als Küchenschrank dient.

This two-story loft was originally no more than the bare shell of an old telephone factory. The entrance, with a guest bathroom, is connected to the upper story by a small staircase, which opens onto a large bathroom that divides the bedrooms from the living area. This bathroom hides various closets, installations and gadgets. The main staircase leads directly to the sitting room and the kitchen, going past a closet-type construction with an overhead television before reaching the kitchen worktop, shadowed by a floating "UFO" that serves both as a lighting unit and a larder.

Au départ, ce loft de deux étages n'était rien d'autre que le bâtiment vide d'une ancienne usine de téléphones. Depuis l'entrée, où se trouve une salle de bain pour les invités, on accède par un petit escalier à l'étage supérieur. Celui-ci s'ouvre sur une grande salle de bain qui sépare les chambres à coucher de la zone habitable. Dans cet espace se cachent aussi divers câbles, appareils et installations. L'escalier principal conduit directement à la salle de séjour et à la cuisine. De là, en laissant derrière soi une sorte d'armoire avec un téléviseur suspendu dans les airs, on accède au plan de travail de la cuisine au dessus duquel un « ovni » flottant fait office de lampe et de placard.

En un principio, este loft de dos plantas no era más que la nave desnuda de una vieja fábrica de teléfonos. Desde la entrada, donde hay un baño para invitados, se accede por una escalerita al piso superior. Éste se abre a un amplio cuarto de baño que separa los dormitorios de la zona habitable. En ese espacio se esconden además diversos trasteros, aparatos e instalaciones. La escalera principal conduce directamente a la sala de estar y la cocina. Desde allí, dejando atrás una construcción a modo de armario con un televisor suspendido en lo alto, se llega a la encimera de la cocina, sobre la que un "ovni" flotante sirve tanto de lámpara como de alacena.

Location: **Kreuzberg**
Architect: **Peanutz Architects**
Photos: **© Thomas Bruns**

Peanutz Architects

Genau an der Grenze zum Bezirk Mitte, aber noch in Kreuzberg gelegen, entstand 1998 ein Neubau mit luxuriösen Wohnungen nach Entwürfen des bekannten Architekten Josep P. Kleihues. 180 m² Wohnfläche und riesige Fensterfronten bieten eine moderne Form, im loftartigen Stile zu wohnen, aber gleichzeitig vom Komfort eines Neubaus zu profitieren. Den Ausblick auf den zentralen Potsdamer Platz sowie den beliebten Gendarmenmarkt kann man auch vom kleinen Balkon aus genießen und spürt so die zentrale Lage. Insgesamt bietet das Gebäude eine anonyme, nüchterne Atmosphäre und die gut isolierten Wände sorgen dafür, dass der Bewohner dieser Wohnung Musik machen kann, ohne seine Nachbarn zu stören.

In 1998 the renowned architect Josep P. Kleihues designed a luxurious apartment block on the border of Mitte, but still in Kreuzberg. The huge floor space (1,950 square foot) and the enormous windows on the facade reproduce the typical features of a loft, but with all the conveniences of modern building techniques. The balcony provides splendid views of the central Potsdamer Platz and the delightful Gendarmenmarkt. The building as a whole looks discreet and unobtrusive, and the excellent soundproofing even allows the inhabitants of this apartment to play music without disturbing their neighbors.

En 1998, le fameux architecte Josep P. Kleihues présente un projet d'appartements luxueux à Kreuzberg, à coté même du prestigieux quartier de Berlin Mitte, qui connaît actuellement un nouvel essor. Ces appartements, qui font 180 m² de superficie et qui sont pourvus d'immenses baies vitrées sur toute une façade, proposent à la manière d'un loft, un espace moderne où l'on peut apprécier toutes les commodités d'une nouvelle construction. Le balcon, offre une vue imprenable sur la place centrale de Postdam et sur le charmant marché des Gendarmes. Dans l'ensemble, le bâtiment semble anonyme et sobre. Aussi, le bon isolement des murs permet aux habitants de pouvoir jouer de la musique sans déranger le voisinage.

Situado en el barrio de Kreuzberg aunque en el borde mismo del barrio de Mitte, el prestigioso arquitecto Josep P. Kleihues proyectó en 1998 un edificio de viviendas de lujo. Los 180 m² de superficie con enormes ventanales en la fachada ofrecen un habitáculo moderno a modo de loft pero dotado de todas las comodidades de la construcción nueva. Las céntricas vistas sobre la plaza de Potsdam y el encantador Mercado de los Gendarmes se disfrutan también desde el balconcito. En conjunto, el edificio ofrece una imagen anónima y sobria, y el buen aislamiento de las paredes permite que los moradores de esta vivienda puedan incluso tocar música sin molestar a sus vecinos.

Location: **Kreuzberg / Mitte**
Architect: **Josep P. Kleihues**
Photos: **© concrete**

Loft Charlottenstraße

Josep P. Kleihues

Dieses nur 50 m² große Apartment befindet sich im zentralen Bezirk Kreuzberg. Das Haus wurde 1997 im Rahmen des sozialen Wohnungsbaus errichtet und so braucht man für die Anmietung einer Wohneinheit auch einen Wohnberechtigungsschein (erhältlich für Leute mit geringeren Einkünften). Die großen, bis zum Boden reichenden Fenster sorgen für viel Licht und eine helle und freundliche Atmosphäre. Bei der Einrichtung wurden Originalobjekte aus den 60er und 70er Jahren, wie z. B. das Sofa, die Deckenlampen im Wohn- und Schlafzimmerbereich und der Gitterstuhl in der Küche, mit praktischen modernen Einrichtungsgegenständen kombiniert.

This small apartment (a mere 535 square foot) is situated in the central Kreuzberg neighbourhood, in a public housing building completed in 1997. The homes inside can only be rented on production of a certificate exclusively available to people on a low income. The big windows, which stretch down to the floor, provide abundant light and create a pleasant and luminous atmosphere. The decoration combines practical modern pieces with original items from the 60s and 70s, including the sofa, the lamps on the ceilings in the lounge and bedrooms and the latticed chair in the kitchen.

Ce petit appartement de seulement 50 m² se trouve dans le quartier de Kreuzberg, dans un bâtiment construit en 1997 et officiellement protégé. De ce fait, pour pouvoir louer un appartement dans cet immeuble, il faut avoir un certificat prouvant de faibles revenus. Les grandes baies vitrées qui arrivent jusqu'au sol offrent beaucoup de lumière et créent un espace diaphane agréable. Pour ce qui est de la décoration, des objets originaux des années 60 et 70, comme le canapé, les lampes qui décorent le plafond du salon et des chambres, ou encore la chaise en cannage de la cuisine, sont associés à d'autres objets modernes et pratiques.

Este pequeño apartamento de sólo 50 m² se encuentra en el céntrico barrio de Kreuzberg, en un edificio de protección oficial construido en 1997. Por ello, para poder alquilar una de las viviendas se necesita un certificado que sólo obtienen personas con ingresos bajos. Los grandes ventanales que llegan hasta el suelo proporcionan mucha luz y crean un ambiente diáfano y agradable. En la decoración se combinan objetos originales de los años 60 y 70, como otros el sofá, las lámparas que ornamentan el techo de la sala y los dormitorios y la silla de rejilla de la cocina, con prácticas piezas modernas.

Location: **Kreuzberg**
Design: **By the resident**
Photos: **© concrete**

Mini-apartment

By the resident

Das am Ende des 19. Jahrhunderts errichtete Gebäude diente zunächst als Stabs-Direktionsgebäude der preußischen Kasernen. Später wurde die Wohnung zum vorübergehenden Domizil des letzten Reichskanzlers Paul Hindenburg und Mitte der 80er Jahre Teil der Internationalen Bauaustellung (IBA). In einem Sanierungs- und Restrukturierungsprogramm teilte man die 500 m^2 große Wohnung in drei separate Einheiten auf, wovon sich das Gestalterteam cheval 2.3 eine Nutzfläche von 172 m^2 in loftartigem Stil als Wohnraum und Studio ausgebaut hat. Durch die alten Parkettböden und die holzvertäfelten Türen ist der typische Stil der Gründerzeitwohnungen erhalten geblieben.

This building, put up at the end of the nineteenth century, was originally the headquarters of the Prussian barracks. It was later used as the temporary residence of the last Chancellor of the Reich, Paul Hindenburg, and in the mid-eighties it housed part of the International Building Exhibition (IBA). A program of repairs and restructuring resulted in the division of the 5,400-square foot home into three independent units. In one of these, the creative team cheval 2.3 converted the 1,850-square foot loft into their home and office. The old parquet floor and the wood-paneled doors preserve characteristic features of the Gründerzeit style.

L'immeuble, construit à la fin XIXème siècle, a d'abord été le siège de l'état major des cartels prussiens. Plus tard, il servit de domicile provisoire au dernier chancelier du Reich, Paul Hindenburg, et au milieu des années 80, il accueillit une partie de l'Exposition Internationale de la Construction (IBA). En vertu d'un programme de restructuration et d'assainissement, le logement de 500 m^2 a été divisé en trois parties indépendantes. A partir de là, l'équipe créative cheval 2.3 habilita un loft de 172 m^2 pour en faire une maison et un bureau. L'ancien parquet et les portes de bois font perdurer le style caractéristique du Gründerzeit.

El edificio levantado a finales del XIX fue, en un principio, sede del Estado Mayor de los cuarteles prusianos. Más tarde sirvió de domicilio provisional al último canciller del Reich, Paul Hindenburg, y a mediados de la década de 1980 acogió parte de la Exposición Internacional de la Construcción (IBA). En virtud de un programa de saneamiento y reestructuración, la vivienda de 500 m^2 se dividió en tres unidades independientes. Allí, el equipo creativo cheval 2.3 habilitó un loft de 172 m^2 como vivienda y despacho. El antiguo parquet de madera y las puertas con paneles de madera hacen que perviva el característico estilo Gründerzeit.

In dieser nur 48 m² großen Wohnung lebt der Charme der alten Zeiten und man kann dem schnellen Rhythmus des modernen Berlin für eine Weile entfliehen. Fast scheint es, als ob jeder Zentimeter Wand und Raumfläche eine Geschichte in sich birgt. Die Objekte stammen aus den unterschiedlichsten Epochen und man findet Kitsch, Klassisches, Bauernmöbel etc. bis hin zu religiösen Objekten. Die Farbe an den Wänden wurde mit einer Schwammtechnik auf den zum Teil schon bröckelnden Putz aufgetragen, aber gerade diese Verbindung von alter Baustruktur und eigenwilligem Interieur verleiht der Wohnung ihren ganz eigentümlichen Charakter.

This apartment, occupying a mere 515 square feet, exudes the charm of days gone by, providing a respite from the hubbub of modern Berlin. Every inch of the walls and every table top seem to have a story to tell. The decorative elements come from different periods, with space being found for kitsch, classicism, rustic furniture and even religious objects. The colouring of the wall has been applied by using a sponge on the slightly cracked plaster, and it is precisely this conjunction of the building's old structure with such a striking interior that gives the home its highly distinctive and original personality.

Dans cette demeure de seulement 48 m² perdure l'enchantement de la vielle époque qui permet d'échapper l'espace d'un instant au rythme du Berlin moderne. Chaque centimètre de mur, chaque espace semble renfermer une histoire. Les éléments décoratifs proviennent de différentes époques et le kitsch, le classique, le rustique et même les objets religieux ont leur place. La peinture du mur a été appliquée avec la technique de l'éponge sur le ravalement partiellement lézardé, mais c'est précisément cette union entre l'ancienne structure de la construction et l'intérieur si spécial qui fait tout le charme et l'originalité de la maison.

En esta vivienda de sólo 48 m² pervive el encanto de los viejos tiempos y en ella se puede escapar por un instante del rápido ritmo del Berlín moderno. Cada centímetro de pared, cada superficie, parecen esconder una historia. Los elementos decorativos provienen de diferentes épocas y hay sitio para el kitsch, el estilo clásico, los muebles rústicos e incluso objetos religiosos. El color de la pared se aplicó con la técnica de la esponja sobre el revoque, parcialmente agrietado, pero precisamente esa unión entre la estructura antigua de la construcción y un interior tan especial le dan a la vivienda su peculiar y originalísimo carácter.

Location: **Prenzlauer Berg**
Design: **By the residents**
Photos: © **E. Wentorf**

Potpourri of styles

325

By the residents

1952 beschloss die sozialistische Regierung der DDR, in Ost-Berlin ein architektonisches Manifest des Wiederaufbaus und eine politische Demonstration gegen den westdeutschen Konstruktivismus zu realisieren. Unter dem Leitbild des sowjetischen Städtebaus entstanden zwischen Alexanderplatz und Frankfurter Tor qualitativ hochwertige Gebäude, die einen Gegensatz zu dem sonst üblichen Plattenbau bildeten, unter ihnen die bekannten Turmhäuser am Frankfurter Tor. Die abgebildete Wohnung befindet sich im 6. Stock des Nordturmhauses und verfügt über eine Wohnfläche von 150 m^2 und 6 Zimmer. Das Gebäude wurde 1999/2000 saniert.

In 1952 the Socialist government of the GDR decided to implement a manifesto for architectural reconstruction in East Berlin as a political statement opposing the Constructivism of West Germany. In keeping with the ideals of Soviet city planning, several high-quality buildings, very different from the usual prefabricated blocks, were put up between Alexanderplatz and the Frankfurt Gate. They included the famous Frankfurt Gate skyscraper, which was restored from 1999 to 2000. The 6-room home in the illustration, situated on the sixth floor of the North tower, measures 1,600 square feet.

En 1952, le gouvernement socialiste de la RDA décide de mettre au point à Berlin Est un manifeste architectural de reconstruction ainsi qu'une déclaration politique contre le constructivisme de l'Allemagne Occidentale. En suivant l'idéal d'urbanisme soviétique, on construit entre la Place Alexander et la porte de Francfort divers bâtiments de grande qualité, très différents des habituels blocs préfabriqués. On remarque parmi eux les fameux gratte-ciel de la porte de Francfort. Ce logement, situé au sixième étage de la tour Nord, fait 150 m^2 et dispose de 6 pièces. Le bâtiment à été restauré entre 1999 et 2000.

Corría 1952 cuando el Gobierno Socialista de la RDA decidió llevar a cabo en Berlín Este un manifiesto arquitectónico de reconstrucción y una declaración política contra el constructivismo de la Alemania Occidental. Siguiendo el ideal de urbanismo soviético, entre la plaza Alexander y la Puerta de Frankfurt se levantaron varios edificios de gran calidad, muy diferentes a los bloques prefabricados habituales, de entre los que destacan los famosos rascacielos de la Puerta de Frankfurt. Esta vivienda, situada en un sexto piso de la torre norte, tiene 150 m^2 y seis habitaciones. El edificio fue restaurado entre los años 1999 y 2000.

By the resident

Bei der Einrichtung stand für die Be-
wohnerin und Designerin Barbara
Dechant vor allem die Funktionalität
und der ästhetische Anspruch an ein-
fache und praktische Dinge im Vordergrund.

The designer Barbara Dechant's guiding principle in the conversion were
functionality and her taste for simple,
practical objects.

Lors de la réforme de sa maison, le
designer Barbara Dechant s'est laissé séduire par un mobilier fonction-
nel, à la fois simple et pratique.

En la reforma de su casa, la diseñadora Barbara Dechant se dejó
guiar, sobre todo, por la funcionalidad
y el gusto por las cosas sencillas y
prácticas.

rn dämpfen sie ... ... abschmecken ... ... fla

Die Architektin und Designerin Nany Wiegand-Hoffmann hat bei der Einrichtung ihrer 220 m² großen Altbauwohnung aus der Jahrhundertwende Mobiliar des Europäischen Klassizismus mit Objekten ihrer eigenen Kollektion im modern-klassischen Stile vermischt. Großen Einfluss bei der Formierung ihres eigenen unverwechselbaren Stiles, den sie zugleich als berlinerisch und kosmopolitisch bezeichnet, hatten der Architekt, Designer und Künstler Karl-Friedrich Schinkel sowie ein vierjähriger Aufenthalt in London, wo sie den traditionellen englischen Stil entdeckte. Im Wohnraum schmücken vier Siebdrucke aus ihrer eigenen Kollektion „Berlin Zyklus" die Wand über dem Sofa.

In her 2,370 square foot apartment dating from the turn of the nineteenth century, the architect and designer Nany Wiegand-Hoffman has combined European Classicism with modern pieces from her own collection to create an eclectic, hybrid decor. One crucial influence on her own unmistakable style, which she defines as "Berlin and cosmopolitan at the same time", was the architect, designer and artist Karl-Friedrich Schinkel – not forgetting the four years she lived in London, where she discovered the traditional English style. Four screen prints from her own "Berlin Series" collection adorn the wall over the sofa in the living room.

Cette demeure de 220 m² date de la décennie comprise entre le XIXème et le XXème siècle. L'architecte et designer Nany Wiegand-Hoffman associe à un mobilier classique européen des objets de sa collection particulière. Ce mélange donne une décoration moderno-classique très éclectique. Son style, fort reconnaissable, est défini par elle-même comme « à la fois berlinois et cosmopolite ». Elle a été influencée par l'architecte, le designer et l'artiste Karl-Friedrich Schinkel, ainsi que par les quatre années passées à Londres durant lesquelles elle a découvert le style traditionnel anglais. Dans le salon, quatre sérigraphies de sa collection « Série Berlin » décorent le mur au-dessus du canapé.

La arquitecta y diseñadora Nany Wiegand-Hoffman ha combinado en los 220 m² de su piso, original de la década entre los siglos XIX y XX, mobiliario del clasicismo europeo con objetos de su propia colección en una ecléctica decoración moderno-clásica. Una influencia decisiva en su estilo propio e inconfundible, definido por ella misma como "berlinés y cosmopolita a un tiempo", fue el arquitecto, diseñador y artista Karl-Friedrich Schinkel, además de los cuatro años que residió en Londres, donde descubrió el estilo tradicional inglés. En la sala, cuatro serigrafías de su propia colección "Serie Berlín" adornan la pared sobre el sofá.

Location: **Zehlendorf**
Architect: **Wiegand-Hoffmann**
Photos: © **concrete**

Aristocratic home

341

Wiegand-Hoffmann

In einer kurzen Bauzeit von 8 Monaten entstanden im Jahre 1999 und 2000 im Bezirk Zehlendorf direkt am Königsweg, dem alten königlichen Reitweg von Berlin nach Potsdam, gelegen, 3 Atelierhäuser mit einer Wohnfläche von jeweils 275 m². Die Flächennutzung sollte sowohl auf wohnliche als auch gewerbliche Zwecke ausgelegt sein. Bei der Fassadengestaltung entschied man sich für eine Holzverschalung aus kanadischer Lärche, die mit der Zeit einen dezenten grauen Farbton annehmen wird und dann eine harmonische Einheit mit der Sichtbetonfertigteilwand und den metallisch grauen Flügeln der Holz- und Aluminiumfenster bildet.

Between 1999 and 2000, in just eight months, three workshop-houses with a habitable space of 2,960 square foot, suitable for both domestic and professional use, were built in the Zehlendorf neighbourhood, alongside the Königsweg, the old Royal Road connecting Berlin with Potsdam. Planks made of Canadian larch wood were chosen to clad the facade; over time these will take on a slightly grayish hue to match the color of the prefabricated, exposed concrete walls and the metallic tones of the aluminum and wood window frames.

Entre 1999 et 2000, dans un bref intervalle de 8 mois, trois maisons atelier ont été construites dans le quartier de Zehlendorf, près du Königsweg, l'antique Chemin Royal qui va de Berlin à Potsdam. Chacune de ces maisons fait 275 m² et a été conçue pour proposer un usage aussi bien domestique que professionnel. On a choisi pour la façade un coffrage en bois de mélèze du Canada, qui avec le temps prendra une couleur grise en accord avec la couleur des murs préfabriqués en béton apparent et celle des battants gris métallique des fenêtres en bois et en aluminium.

Apenas ocho meses tardaron en construirse, entre los años 1999 y 2000, en el barrio de Zehlendorf y directamente junto al Königsweg, el viejo Camino Real que lleva de Berlín a Potsdam, tres casas-taller, cada una con una superficie habitable de 275 m², a las que pudiera darse un uso tanto doméstico como profesional. Para la configuración de la fachada se escogió un encofrado de madera de alerce de Canadá, que con el tiempo adquirirá un discreto tono grisáceo acorde con el color de las paredes prefabricadas de hormigón visto y el tono gris metálico de los batientes de las ventanas de madera y aluminio.

Location: **Zehlendorf**
Architect: **Becher + Rottkamp**
Photos: **© concrete**

Workshop-houses

349

Becher + Rottkamp

Diese im Bezirk Tiergarten und direkt am Schöneberger Ufer gelegene Wohnung bietet inmitten des Zentrums von Berlin eine schnelle Flucht ins Grüne und ans Wasser. In den 70er Jahren wurden die riesigen Etagenwohnungen des aus der Jahrhundertwende stammenden Gebäudes in jeweils drei kleinere Wohnungen aufgeteilt. Die heutige Nutzungsfläche von 130 m^2 wurde im minimalistischen Stil der funktionalen Eleganz eingerichtet. Ein gelber Küchenschrank aus Schleiflack, der aus einem Ostberliner Plattenbau stammt, wurde zum Bücherregal umfunktioniert und im Wohnzimmer aufgestellt. Ein angefertigtes Eiche-Regal dient gleichermaßen als Sekretär und Arbeitsplatz wie auch als Musikregal.

This apartment in the Tiergarten neighbourhood, on the canal bank near the Schöneberger Ufer, enjoys the advantages of the natural world in the very heart of Berlin. In the seventies each of the enormous homes in this late-nineteenth-century building was subdivided into three apartments. The resulting floor space of 1,400 square foot was decorated in a minimalist style of functional elegance. A yellow-lacquered closet, rescued from a prefabricated block in East Berlin, has been turned into a bookcase for the living room. More shelves – this time in oak and made to order – serve as a desk, as well as a home for the music system.

Cet appartement, situé dans le quartier de Tiergarten et donnant directement sur la rive de Schöneberger Ufer, permet de profiter de l'eau et de la nature en plein coeur de Berlin. Dans les années 70, chacun des grands logements de cet immeuble qui date de la fin du XIXème siècle, a été divisé en trois appartements. La superficie actuelle est de 130 m^2 et a été décorée dans un style minimaliste et élégant. Un placard de cuisine, récupéré d'un bloc préfabriqué de Berlin Est et laqué en jaune, a été transformé en bibliothèque pour le salon. Une autre étagère, en bois chêne et spécialement commandée pour l'occasion, fait office de secrétaire et de bureau. Elle sert aussi de support à la chaîne haute-fidélité.

Este piso situado en el barrio de Tiergarten, directamente en la ribera de Schöneberger Ufer, permite disfrutar en pleno centro de Berlín del agua y la naturaleza. En los años 70, cada una de las enormes viviendas de este edificio de finales del XIX se subdividió en tres apartamentos. La superficie habitable actual de 130 m^2 fue decorada en un estilo minimalista de funcional elegancia. Un armario de cocina lacado en amarillo, rescatado de un bloque prefabricado del Berlín Este, se reconvirtió en librería para el salón. Otra estantería de roble, expresamente encargada, sirve de secreter y escritorio, y también para colocar el equipo de música.

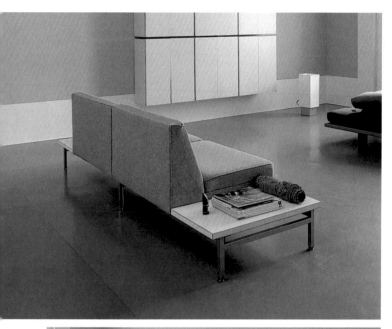

Dieses 350 m² große Loft teilen sich drei Bewohner als Wohn- und Arbeitsraum. Das ehemals gewerblich genutzte Gebäude aus den 20er Jahren wurde im Jahre 1998 saniert. Beim Eigenausbau haben die Bewohner den industriellen Charakter der Räumlichkeiten weitgehend bewahrt. Drei etwa 15 m² große Schlafzimmer wurden von der Raumfläche abgetrennt und stellen so für die Bewohner einen intimen Rückzugsort dar. Mit dem ehemaligen Industriefahrstuhl gelangt man direkt in den Loft, zum Öffnen der Tür braucht man jedoch einen Privatschlüssel. Eine Unbequemlichkeit stellen die sanitären Einrichtungen dar, die sich noch immer als Sammelbäder auf den Fluretagen befinden.

Up to three people share this 3,300 square foot loft as a home and workspace. The old factory, dating from the 1920s, was refurbished in 1998, with the aim of preserving the industrial character of the building as far as possible. Three bedrooms – occupying some 160 square foot and separate from the common living space – provide an intimate retreat for each of the inhabitants. The industrial elevator, which has been retained, leads directly to the entrance of the loft but the door can only be opened with a key. The toilets involve a degree of inconvenience as they are in the corridor, in a bathroom for communal use.

Trois personnes habitent dans ce loft de 350 m², qui sert à la fois de logement et de lieu de travail. La rénovation du hangar, appartenant à une usine des années 20, a été réalisée en 1998. Lors des travaux, on a conservé le caractère industriel du bâtiment. Les trois chambres de 15 m² sont toutes séparées du reste de l'espace commun. Elles offrent un lieu d'intimité aux occupants. Le monte-charge industriel a été conservé et conduit directement à l'entrée du loft. Néanmoins, la porte se ferme à clef. Les toilettes présentent un petit inconvénient du fait qu'ils sont sur le palier et sont par conséquent communautaires.

Este loft de 350 m² es compartido y utilizado por tres personas como vivienda y lugar de trabajo. La reforma de la antigua nave de una fábrica de los años 20 se llevó a cabo en 1998. En la remodelación se intentó conservar en lo posible el carácter industrial del edificio. Separados del resto del espacio habitable común, tres dormitorios de unos 15 m² cada uno constituyen el lugar de retiro e intimidad de los habitantes. El montacargas industrial, que se ha conservado, conduce directamente a la entrada del loft pero la puerta se abre sólo con llave. Los lavabos constituyen una pequeña incomodidad, ya que se encuentran en el pasillo a modo de baño comunitario.

Location: **Wedding**
Architect: **Hartgelb Gruppe**
Photos: © **Hendrik Blaukat**

Loft Wedding

Hartgelb Gruppe

Dieser 335 m² große Altbau bietet ausreichend Raum, um sowohl als Wohnort, Atelier als auch als Ausstellungsraum zu dienen. Die Wohnung hat neun Zimmer und die Übergänge der verschiedenen Nutzungsflächen sind fließend. Bei der Renovierung im Jahre 1999/2000 wurde der klassisch herrschaftliche Stil zum großen Teil erhalten, aber mit modernen Elementen kombiniert. So wurde die aus dem Jahre 1904 stammende Stuckdecke wieder freigelegt und die unterschiedlichen alten Parkettböden abgezogen und versiegelt. Die Kunstwerke sowie modernen Installationen stammen von Peter oder Annette Buecheler selbst und werden in den regelmäßigen hauseigenen Ausstellungen, sogenannten „Kunstsalons", zur Schau gestellt.

This enormous old apartment, measuring 4,120 square feet, provides enough space for a home, workshop and art gallery, with 9 rooms that are fluidly interconnnected. The conversion, carried out from 1999 to 2000, respected the classic aristocratic style while introducing modern features. So, the original stucco roof, dating from 1904, was restored and the old parquet floors were sanded down and varnished. The modern paintings and installations are the work of Peter and Annette Buecheler, and they are put on show in the exhibitions regularly held in the apartment's very own "art salon".

Cet ancien appartement de 335 m² a un espace tel qu'il permet d'accueillir un logement, un atelier et une salle d'exposition. La maison se compose de 9 pièces qui communiquent entre elles avec fluidité. Lors des travaux, réalisés entre 1999 et 2000, on a préservé le style seigneurial classique tout en le combinant avec des éléments modernes. On a ainsi pu conserver le plafond en stuc datant de 1904 et on a récupéré l'ancien parquet en le ponçant et en le colmatant. Les oeuvres d'art et les installations modernes sont de Peter et Annette Buecheler et peuvent être admirées lors des expositions périodiquement célébrées dans la « salle d'art » de la maison.

Este enorme piso antiguo de 335 m² ofrece espacio suficiente para acoger una vivienda, un taller y una sala de exposiciones. La casa tiene nueve habitaciones comunicadas entre sí de forma fluida. En la reforma, llevada a cabo entre los años 1999 y 2000, se respetó el estilo señorial clásico, combinado, eso sí, con elementos modernos. De esta forma, se recuperó el techo estucado original de 1904 y se acuchillaron y sellaron los suelos de parquet antiguo. Las obras de arte y las instalaciones modernas son de Peter y Annette Buecheler y se muestran en las exposiciones celebradas periódicamente en la "sala de arte" de la propia casa.

By the residents

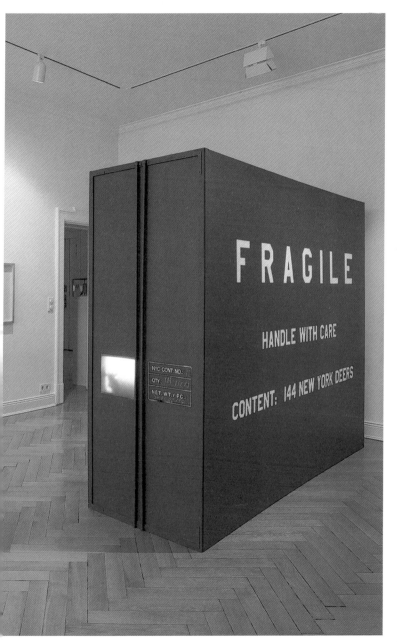

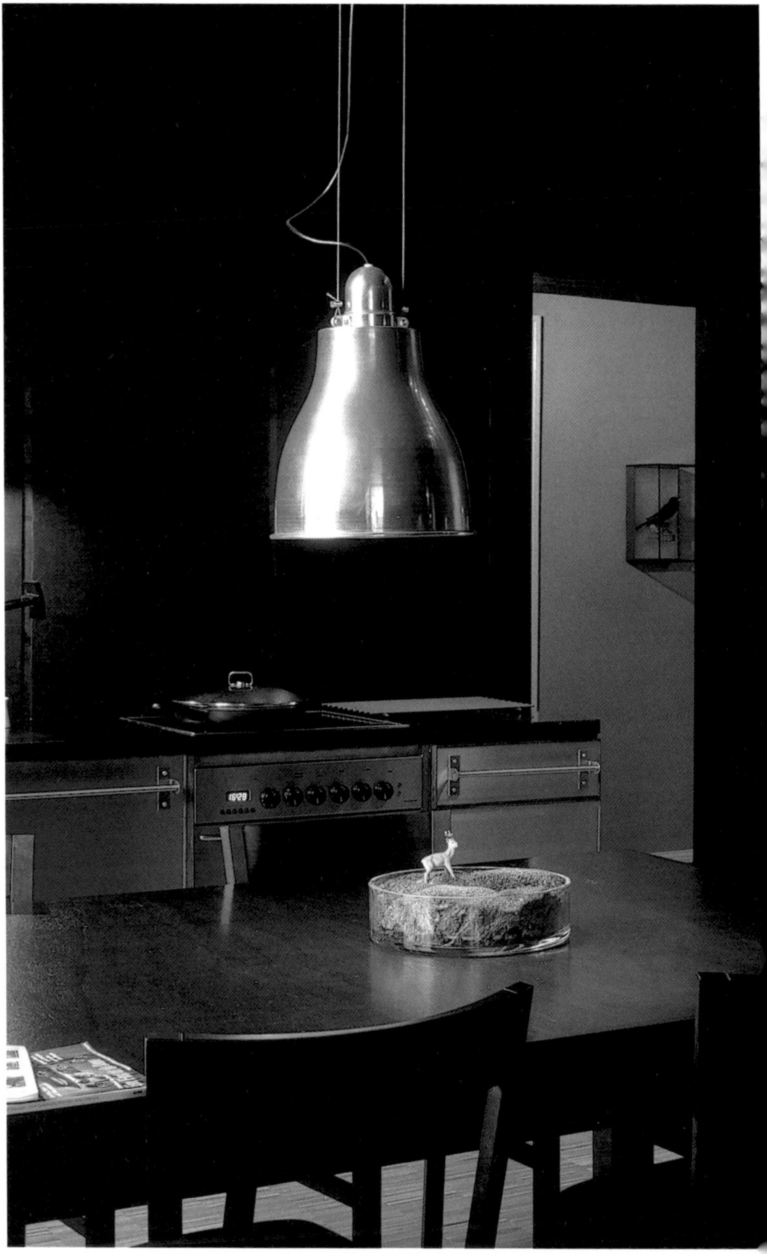

Die vier herrschaftlichen Räume dieser Wohnung im grünen Stadtrandgebiet Grunewald wurden mit Möbeln und Bildern der verschiedensten Stil- und Kunstgattungen dekoriert. Im lichtdurchfluteten, romantischen Wintergarten thront ein kostbarer Rosenquarzleuchter über einem selbstentworfenen Esstisch im Renaissance-Stil und im ehemaligen holzverkleideten Herrenzimmer, welches heute als Schlafzimmer dient, wurde ein Bild des englischen Popart-Künstlers Allen Jones mit einem antiken Portraitbild von Philippine Charlotte, der Schwester des Preußenkönigs Friedrich des Großen, kombiniert. Im Wohnzimmer steht eine wertvolle Art-déco-Sitzgruppe.

This apartment's four majestic rooms in the leafy neighbourhood of Grunewald, on the outskirts of the city, are decorated with furniture and paintings with various themes and styles. The luminous, romantic conservatory is dominated by a valuable pink quartz chandelier hanging over a dining-table designed by the owner in a style inspired by the Renaissance. In the original study, clad with wooden panels and now used as a bedroom, a painting by the Pop artist Allen Jones hangs next to an old portrait of Philippine Charlotte, the sister of Frederick the Great, the king of Prussia. The sitting room boasts a valuable set of Art Deco chairs.

Les quatre pièces seigneuriales de cette maison, située dans le quartier verdoyant de Grunewald, sont décorées à l'aide de meubles et de tableaux de styles et de mouvements artistiques divers. Dans le lumineux et romantique jardin d'hiver, trône au dessus d'une table de salle à manger style Renaissance, un impérieux lustre de quartz rose. Dans l'ancien boudoir du maître de maison recouvert de panneaux de bois et qui sert aujourd'hui de chambre à coucher, se trouve à côté d'un tableau de l'artiste pop anglais Allen Jones, un vieux portrait de Philippine Charlotte, sœur de Frédéric le Grand, roi de Prusse. On trouve dans le séjour une importante série de chaises Arts Déco.

Estilos y géneros diversos se mezclan en los muebles y cuadros que decoran las cuatro habitaciones señoriales de esta vivienda del verde barrio de Grunewald, en las afueras. En el luminoso y romántico invernáculo impera una valiosa lámpara de cuarzo de rosa sobre una mesa de comedor de diseño propio inspiradas en el renacimiento. En el antiguo gabinete del señor de la casa, revestido con paneles de madera y que hoy se utiliza como dormitorio, se colgó un cuadro del artista pop inglés Allen Jones junto a un retrato antiguo de Philippine Charlotte, hermana de Federico el Grande, rey de Prusia. En la sala hay un valioso grupo de sillas arts decó.

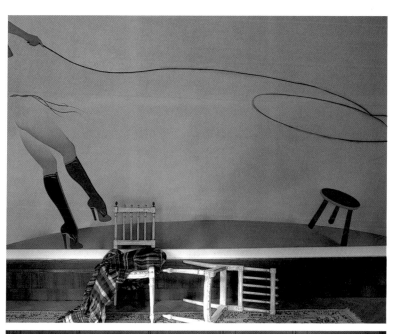

In Zusammenarbeit mit Innenarchitekt Stefan Poth entwickelte sich die Idee für dieses 250 m² große Wohnhaus. Ein besonderes Interesse galt der Gestaltung des Treppenhauses, dessen Glasschneise den rustikalen Trakt aus Sichtbeton und rauen Zedernholzbrettern vom weiß verputzten Baukörper trennt. Raumhohe Schiebetüren verknüpfen die verschiedenen Nutzungsbereiche. Die Böden im Eingangs-, Ess- und Küchenbereich sind aus grauem Granit, während man sich im Wohnraum für Parkettdielen entschied. In der Achse des Treppenhauses liegt im Außenbereich im Süden das Schwimmbecken, welches von Sonnenkollektoren auf dem Dach beheizt wird.

The concept for this 2,700 square foot house was developed in conjunction with the interior decorator Stefan Poth. Special attention was paid to the staircase, with a sheet of glass that divides the rustic, exposed concrete section with cedar panels from the main whitewashed architectural structure. The sliding doors that stretch to the ceiling unify the various rooms. The floor in the entrance, dining room and kitchen is made of gray granite, while floorboards were chosen for the sitting room. Outside, under the axis of the staircase, the swimming pool faces south, heated with the energy supplied by the solar panels in the roof.

La conceptualisation de cette maison de 250 m² s'est faite en collaboration avec le décorateur Stefan Poth. On a accordé un intérêt tout particulier à l'escalier, où une plaque en verre sépare la structure rustique de béton apparent et les planches non polies en bois de cèdre, du corps architectural peint en blanc. Les portes coulissantes qui arrivent jusqu'au plafond unissent les différents espaces. Le sol de l'entrée, de la salle à manger et de la cuisine est en granit grisâtre tandis qu'on a choisi du parquet pour le salon. A l'extérieur, sous l'axe de l'escalier, la piscine climatisée est orientée vers le sud et puise son énergie des panneaux solaires installés sur le toit.

El concepto de esta casa de 250 m² se desarrolló en colaboración con el decorador Stefan Poth. Especial interés se prestó a la escalera, con una placa de cristal que separa la estructura rústica de hormigón visto y bastas tablas de cedro del cuerpo arquitectónico revocado en blanco. Las puertas correderas que se alzan hasta el techo unen los diferentes habitáculos. El suelo de la entrada, el comedor y la cocina es de granito grisáceo, mientras que para el salón se eligió un entarimado. En el exterior, bajo el eje de la escalera, la piscina climatizada está orientada hacia el sur y se alimenta de los paneles de energía solar del tejado.

Location: **Reinickendorf**
Architect: **Peter P. Pabel**
Photos: © **Wini Sulzbach**

Wittenau house

Peter P. Pabel

Other Designpocket titles by teNeues:

Cafés & Restaurants 3-8238-5478-X

Cool Hotels 3-8238-5556-5

Country Hotels 3-8238-5574-3

Exhibition Design 3-8238-5548-4

Furniture/Möbel/Meubles/Mobile Design 3-8238-5575-1

Italian Interior Design 3-8238-5495-X

London Apartments 3-8238-5558-1

Los Angeles Houses 3-8238-5594-8

New York Apartments 3-8238-5557-3

Office Design 3-8238-5578-6

Paris Apartments 3-8238-5571-9

Product Design 3-8238-5597-2

Showrooms 3-8238-5496-8

Spa & Wellness Hotels 3-8238-5595-6

Staircases 3-8238-5572-7

Tokyo Houses 3-8238-5573-5

Each volume:

12.5 x 18.5 cm
400 pages
c. 450 color illustrations